Simple Home Cooking

Jams

Preserves, Chutneys & Curds

Publisher & Creative Director: Nick Wells
Senior Project Editor: Marcus Hardy
Art Director: Mike Spender
Layout Design: Jane Ashley
Digital Design & Production: Chris Herbert
Proofreader: Dawn Laker

Special thanks to Lydia Good for editorial and picture research assistance.

This is a **FLAME TREE** Book

FLAME TREE PUBLISHING
Crabtree Hall, Crabtree Lane
Fulham, London SW6 6TY
United Kingdom
www.flametreepublishing.com

Flame Tree is part of Flame Tree Publishing Limited

First published 2012

Images courtesy of the following: **shutterstock** and © the following photographers: front cover Christopher Elwell; 9 yuris; 10 Julija Sapic;
11 Linda Macpherson; 12 Lilyana Vynogradova; 13 Christian Jung; 14 Grzegorzgodlewski; 15 n333; 16 Joe Gough; 18 JinYoung Lee; 19 Ev Thomas; 21
Gayvoronskaya_Yana; 22 Stefan Fierros; 23 Baldwin; 34 Marcio Jose Bastos Silva; 35 Ann Baldwin; 30 Timmary; 31 Juri; 33 Lucy
Bratwustle; 47 Digivic; 49 Chezlov; 51 K & W; 55 HLPhoto; 57 Mahas; 59 Christopher Elwell; 62 Skyline; 63 Bratwustle; 65 Cgissemann;
69 marco mayer; 71 gosphotodesign; 73 Anjelagr; 81 Dusha Petrenko; 83 Zanetti Berishkumar; 85 Stephanie Fray ; 86–7 Larry Munday;
91 Dirk Ott; 93 Christian Jung ; 95 Heike Rau; 97 Peños; 99 Tomasz Wiejo; 101 Olga Utvakova; 105 Bronwyn Photo; 107 avs; 109
Foodpictures; 111 MSPhotographic; 119 Nedim Jukić; 121 rsphoto; 129 Subbotina Anna;
131 Joerg Beuge; 133 sasmis; 139 cardiae; 141 Piotr Marcinski; 145 Subbotina Anna; 147 Quanthem; 148–9 Gudrun Muenz; 151
LiilyanaVynogradova; 153 monticello; 155 Tobik; 157 Jorg Brandhuber; 163 Ukrainianoveg; 165 Schoenrock; 167 bonchan; 169
ER_09; 170–71 Sayanski; 173 Elena Schweitzer; 185 sarsmis; 189 sarsmis; 191
Dudakova Elena; 193 Sally Wallis; 195 Volker Reusch; 198–9 Nataliya Hora; 201 Wikki; 207 Mona Makela; 207 Jdpictures; 209 Monkey Business
Images; 211 oksix; 213 Mauro Pezzotta ; 217 Photosiber; 225 sarsmis; 231 sarsmis;
233 Gordon Bell; 237 Neil Roy Johnson; 239 ; 249 Neveshkin Nikolay; 251
Elke Dennis; 253 Monkey Business Images; ; 77 Steven Lee; 115 Zen
Shui/Laurence Mouton; 117 Kevin Summers; 229 Lew Robertson; and Lippert; **iStock Photo** and
© the following photographers: 89 Linda; 187 Vishwanath Bhat; 205 PaulMaguire

Simple Home Cooking

Jams

Preserves, Chutneys & Curds

**FLAME TREE
PUBLISHING**

Contents

☙

Ingredients and Equipment

It is hard to explain the pleasure of serving a meal with a homemade jam or preserve. And then there is the joy of seeing a row of homemade preserve jars when you open a cupboard in your kitchen. Whether a jam, jelly, chutney or pickle, there really is nothing better. Making your own preserves also ensures that you can control the quality of the ingredients and that there are no artificial additives.

A Few Basic Rules

Before you start on the road to success, there are a few rules that, if observed, will make life easier and ensure perfect results every time.

- The first rule is to ensure that all the ingredients are in perfect condition. If you have either under- or overripe fruit that you wish to use, it is better to mix the two together. That way, the underripe fruit will give a good amount of pectin while the overripe fruit has the colour and flavour. But it is a juggling act to get the correct balance. Do not use rotten or badly damaged fruit or vegetables or those that look as though they are going bad, as this may taint the finished taste.

- Prepare your produce, washing it thoroughly or peeling thinly, discarding the skin and pips if required by the recipe. Cut the fruit or vegetables into equal-sized pieces. Remember, in marmalade, the skin and pips are used but not the bitter white pith, which is discarded.

- Ensure you have all the ingredients and tools before starting.

- Do not use copper, brass or iron pots and utensils, as the acid in the fruit will react with the metal and spoil the finished result.

Equipment Needed

It is not strictly necessary to buy special equipment for making preserves, but if you plan to make a few, there are some pieces that will make life a little bit easier.

∾ **Large Pan** - choose a pan 7 litres/10 pints in capacity and with a lid. This will come in useful when simmering fruit and vegetables that need a long cooking time. If using this kind of pan for preserving, as well as cooking the produce to soften it, then the preserve will take longer to reach setting point, as the surface area is not as large.

∾ **Preserving Pan** - large pan about 8.5 litres/15 pints with graduated sides and a very wide diameter. Best with a nonreactive interior such as stainless steel, enamel or nonstick. The wide diameter enables evaporation when making the jam, jelly or marmalade, which is boiled vigorously in order to reach setting point.

Use a large pan for jam, jelly or marmalade. The mixture should only half-fill the pan once the sugar has dissolved, otherwise there is a danger of it boiling over onto the hob.

∾ **Long-handled Wooden Spoon** - an essential piece of equipment that enables the successful stirring of the fruit or vegetables. The long handle ensures that the spoon does not fall into the hot liquid. Look for wooden spoons that are at least 30.5 cm/12 ins. Better still are those that are 38 cm/15 ins.

- **Long-handled Slotted Spoon** - these are essential for skimming off any stones or scum that float to the top when boiling to setting point.

- **Jam or Sugar Thermometer** - when making jam, jelly or marmalade, the hot liquid needs to be brought to setting point, 105°C/220°F. You can of course try the saucer method, but the thermometer gives a more accurate reading. Brush the thermometer with warm water and a pastry brush so it remains clean and easy to read.

- **Jelly Bag and Stand** - this is for straining the juices from the fruit pulp after simmering slowly to extract all the liquid possible. The juice is then boiled with sugar to make the jelly. It is possible to improvise a jelly bag and stand by suspending a jelly bag or muslin from the legs of an upturned chair or stool. If using a bought stand, it should be attached to the sides of a large, scalded kitchen bowl such as Pyrex. (The bowl needs scalding to remove any trace of grease or washing up liquid). Pour boiling water into items needing to be scalded. It is essential that the jelly bag be scalded with boiling water before using and the fruit and juice should be left in a draught-free place and not squeezed, in order to allow all the juice to drip through naturally. This will ensure a cloud-free jelly. Wash thoroughly after use and scald each time.

- **Funnel** - this has a wide neck and sits comfortably in the neck of a jam jar, allowing the warm jars to be filled with a minimum of spillage.

- **Slicer** - this can be either an attachment to a freestanding mixer or a table-top slicer, which is clamped to the table top. Many food processors have a slicing attachment. This is a very useful tool for making marmalade. The peel of the Seville oranges is far tougher than other

Equipment Needed

citrus fruits and it needs to be shredded either finely or in chunks to make the marmalade palatable. Some recipes soak the shredded peel for a long period or simmer for 30 minutes covered with water before using in the preserve. The peel can be cut into fine shreds with a sharp kitchen knife, but this can be time-consuming. A slicer takes the hard work out of this job.

- **Cherry Stoner** - useful when making preserves with fresh cherries, it will help to prevent the hands from being stained with the cherry juice. Often a garlic press is a cherry stoner as well.

- **Muslin or Cheesecloth** - ideal to use when needing small bags for whole spices such as star anise or whole cloves to use as flavouring. Can also be used when making marmalade and needing to use the citrus peel and pips. The size will be governed by the amount to be tied up. Also used as a jelly bag. Place the spices or pips in the centre of a double piece of muslin and fold up into a pouch. Tie with a long piece of string and attach to one of the preserving pan handles. Ensure that the bag is immersed in the liquid. Easy to remove at the end of cooking.

- **Sieve** - if you need to use a sieve, ensure that it is nylon to avoid any tainting of the food. Metal could discolour the fruits.

Jars, Pots and Covers

Clean jars are an essential part of preserving. A good habit to get into is to save jars and their lids from commercial products. They must be scrupulously clean and sterilised before use. When required, wash well in hot, soapy water and rinse thoroughly in very hot water to remove all traces of soap. Dry off in a warm oven – this will sterilise the jars. Place upturned jars on a baking sheet in the warm oven 140°C/275°F/Gas Mark 1 for 15 minutes. Place the sterilised jars upside down on a clean tea towel until required. Leave the jam, jelly or marmalade, once setting point has been reached, to stand for 5-10 minutes before potting. Fill the jars while warm. Any warm and sterilised glass jars can be used.

- Preserving Jars - it is possible to buy jars that are specifically designed for preserving. They have a wide neck, making it easier to pack the jars with the vegetables or fruit. Often the lid is attached and has a rubber seal, which ensures that the jar is completely airtight.

- Jam-pot Covers - once made, jellies, marmalades and chutneys should be covered immediately with a small. waxed disc and left until completely cold, then wipe the filled jar with a damp, clean cloth to remove any spillage down the sides of the jar. Cover with lightly dampened cellophane covers and secure with an elastic band or use the sterilised lid of the jar.

Filling Jars

When the jam, jelly or chutney is ready to be potted, place sterilised warm jars on a chopping board, making sure they are not touching. Place a funnel in the jar, then fill a heatproof jug with the hot jam or jelly and pour into the jar, filling to within 1 cm/$^1/_2$ inch of the neck. Cover as above. Label clearly and store in a cool, dark place. Where vinegar is used, the jars must not have a metallic lid.

Equipment Needed

Testing the Jam

- **Testing for a Set** - when testing for a set, draw the pan off the heat while testing. Otherwise, if the jam is still boiling vigorously, the setting point will be missed, as the mixture will be overboiled. This will result in a syrupy consistency, which does not set solidly. The easiest way to test for a set is with a jam/sugar thermometer. Boil the jam vigorously and place the thermometer into the jam after about 5 minutes to get an idea of the temperature. When you think the thermometer has reached 105°C/220°F simply draw the pan off the heat and check it. If the temperature has not been reached, return to a rapid boil and continue to test until the temperature is reached. Remember to brush the thermometer occasionally with water so that you can see the correct temperature.

- **Saucer Test** - place 3-4 saucers in the refrigerator when beginning to boil. When the preserve has been rapidly boiling and is looking thicker, place a small teaspoon of the mixture on a cold saucer and leave for a couple of minutes. Take the pan off the heat when testing for a set. If the jam wrinkles when a clean finger is pushed across the surface of the jam or the sauce, then the setting point has been reached. If it is not ready, return to a rolling boil and retest in a few minutes. Take care not to overboil, otherwise the preserve may caramelise and can burn. Allow the boiled mixture, once the setting point has been reached, to stand for 5-10 minutes before pouring through the funnel into the warm, sterilised jars. This will allow most of the scum (if any) to be removed with the slotted spoon and ensure that, in the case of marmalade or jam with pieces of fruit, the peel or fruit will not float to the top and is evenly distributed.

- **Flake Test** - when the jam has been boiling for about 12 minutes, dip a clean wooden spoon into the jam and twirl it around a little to cool. If it is ready, the jam will partially set on the spoon and drops will run together to form flakes.

- **Volume Testing** - to test how much jam will be made from a given amount of ingredients. (From 1.5 kg/3 lb of sugar, 5 x 450 g/1 lb should be obtained.) To use the volume of jam method, first fill a 450 g/ 1 lb jam jar with water and then pour the water into a clean preserving pan. Ensure that the pan is level. Place a wooden spoon upright into the pan and mark on the spoon the level of the water. Pour the water away and make the jam. When the jam is ready to be tested, remove from the heat and place on a level surface. Place the marked wooden spoon in the jam. When the jam has boiled down to the mark on the spoon, then it is ready to be potted. If you are making 4.5 kg/10 lb of jam, the same method applies but using 10 jam jars. Alternatively, you can use 600 ml/1 pint measurements. Do exactly as above but marking a clean wooden spoon with a 600 ml/1 pint mark.

- **Full Rolling Boil** - this is when the sugar has dissolved and the mixture is brought to the boil and boils rapidly to reach setting point. Take care, as the mixture will rise in the pan almost over the top; this is why a large pan is required. Adding a small knob of butter when bringing the jam to the boil will help to disperse the scum which occurs and rises to the surface.

Ingredients ~ Fruit

℘

Fruit needs to be ripe but still firm, without any rotten or bad pieces. Discard any mushy, overripe, rotten fruits, as this will affect the keeping quality and taste of the finished product. Fruits need to be as fresh as possible and with some, such as Seville oranges, which are in the shops for a very short time, it is possible to freeze them and use later. Seville oranges are seasonal and only appear in the shops around the end of January. Buy and freeze immediately, then use once thawed when time allows. Only keep in the freezer for up to 6 months. When using for marmalade, use a little extra than the recipe says, to allow for any loss of pectin while frozen. Most fruits are ideal for jams and jellies, but there are subtle differences in how they are used.

∾ Cooking Apples - the best cooking apple is the Bramley and it is grown in the UK solely for cooking purposes. It has white flesh, which on cooking fluffs up and makes a perfect purée. It is the balance of sweetness and malic acid in the apple that gives the sharp, tangy, sweet flavour. Although there are other varieties of cooking apple, they are not readily available. Often Granny Smiths are used but the result is not as good. Eating apples are not suitable for cooking, as they do not break down and the flesh becomes slightly rubbery. Cooking apples are perfect in jams, jelly-making and for chutneys and pickles.

∾ Blackberries - a late-summer to early-autumn fruit, grown wild in the hedgerows, and commonly referred to as Brambles. These tend to be smaller than cultivated berries.

The large cultivated varieties can be eaten raw and are ideal when used in pies and other desserts. While the Bramble is used for jams and jellies, care must be taken, as the bushes have many thorns. Available during the summer and early autumn, it is also a good fruit to freeze or preserve for use during the winter months.

- **Cherries** - cherries have pleased the palates of many over the centuries. Their ruby-red colour and tangy taste were first appreciated by the Romans, Ancient Greeks and the Chinese. Cherries were first brought to Italy in the 1600s, and their appeal quickly spread. They have a very short season and out-of-season cherries are only available canned. There are two types of cherries: sweet cherries and sour cherries. The sweet varieties are normally eaten raw, while the sour varieties, such as Morel, are normally cooked, either canned or in a liqueur such as Kirsch. Grown in the US, France and the UK, most of them are varying shades of red. There is also a white cherry called White Heart, or Rainer, which has a pale, creamy skin with hints of red and a yellow/creamy flesh. Cherries are a difficult crop to grow commercially and for economic reasons not many countries grow cherries for export. Most of the varieties are normally grown to be eaten. Other varieties of cherries are Maraschino and Bing.

- **Crab Apples** - these grow wild in the Northern Hemisphere and produce small, marked fruit that is too tart to eat on its own. Like the cultivated apple, the tree is covered with pretty white/pink blossom which needs pollinating in the spring in order to produce fruit, The fruit is not edible raw as it is too small and tart, but it is perfect for jam and jellies.

- **Blueberries** - have only recently been readily available in this country and are grown extensively in North America. Available, thanks to imports, nearly all year round. A small, very dark purple berry, they can be eaten raw or lightly stewed.

Ingredients ~ Fruit

∾ Citrus Fruits - a family of fruit, all of which have a high pectin content and set well. They can be used with other fruits to make many different-flavoured marmalades. There are at least eight different varieties of fruit in the citrus family with variants in each variety.

∾ Seville Orange - classified as a 'bitter' orange, and used primarily for marmalade, as they have very rough and pit-marked skin and an extremely bitter flavour. They can be used in savoury dishes, but use with care - it would be better to use marmalade, otherwise the dish may be spoilt due to bitterness. The other 'bitter' orange is the 'bergamot', grown mainly for its perfume and aroma and essential oils. Grown in China and Southeast Asia.

∾ Orange - available all year round and in different sizes. Some, such as Navel oranges, are large, sweet and normally pipless. Grown extensively in Spain, Florida, Israel and South Africa, they are mainly consumed fresh, although their flavour in the form of zest is used in both sweet and savoury dishes.

∾ Grapefruit - yellow, pink or ruby-red varieties are eaten mainly fresh. The yellow variety is sharper in flavour than the other two. Again, grown in Florida, Texas, South Africa and the West Indies, as well as Southeast Asia. Often eaten raw for breakfast, they can be bought canned. They can also be used for marmalade.

∾ Clementine - regarded by some to be a cross between a tangerine and a sweet orange or as a variety of tangerine. Often pipless.

∾ Satsuma - similar to a tangerine with a loose, floppy skin for easy peeling and containing few pips. Mainly eaten fresh.

~ **Mandarin and Tangerine** - thought by many to be the same small fruit. Easy to peel and eaten fresh or even preserved in a brandy- or other liqueur-flavoured syrup. Grown extensively in Florida, China, Southeast Asia, Spain and South Africa, The tangerine has been used over the years to experiment and produce new varieties.

~ **Kumquat** - a small, oval fruit that has a skin that is sweeter than its flesh. Has a large proportion of pips in relation to its size. Used simply sliced, mainly as decoration, or can be used in chutneys. Grown on small, slow-growing shrubs or small trees. Originates from China.

~ **Pomelo** - the largest of the citrus family, it has a thick, rough skin, white pith and bitter, pulpy flesh - it is normally eaten by itself.

~ **Ugli Fruit** - a large, rough-skinned fruit, a cross between a grapefruit and a tangerine. Native to the West Indies and eaten like a grapefruit.

~ **Lemon** - this is a well-used fruit and can be found throughout the world. Grown in cold climates such as the UK in conservatories and greenhouses. Used in many different ways, both in sweet and savoury dishes, as well as a good source of pectin for jams and jellies. These days, as with all citrus fruits, it is recommended that organic or unwaxed fruits are used to avoid the ingestion of chemicals. If not available, scrub thoroughly before using.

∾ Lime - another popular citrus fruit used in both sweet and savoury dishes. It has a slightly more acidic flavour and they are often not as juicy as lemons. The fruit has a thin skin. A handy tip to extract the juice is to heat on high in a microwave for about 30 seconds, allow to cool, then cut in half to remove the juice.

∾ Currant - there are four varieties; black, red and, more unusually, white, with pink being the most rare. The English word 'currant' dates back to the 1500s, but they were also called 'ribes'. They are now grown in Europe and northern California. They have a short season so it is best to buy and freeze. They are ideal for jam- and jelly-making or summer desserts such as Summer Pudding. Currants, especially red ones, can be rather tart, so are not normally eaten raw. All are perfect for making jellies for serving with roast meat and other savoury dishes. Blackcurrants form the basis of Cassis, the well-known French liqueur. To prepare, currants are normally stripped from their stalks with a fork.

∾ Date - these are one of the super foods. Available both fresh and dried. They have been around for more than 8,000 years. They are grown mainly in Israel and North Africa and vary in colour from honey-yellow to red to brown. It is these brown dates we are most familiar with. Dried dates are available all year round, fresh dates are around from November to January and in the summer months. They have a high quantity of natural sugar, with a slightly chewy texture, with the Medjool date being the best known and most widely available. Dried dates are available in boxes, in blocks or chopped and rolled in sugar to prevent them sticking together.

∾ Fig - it is believed that figs were first grown in Greece in 8000 BC and later also in Spain, Portugal and North Africa. From there, they spread to the rest of Europe and by the 17th century to North America and Australia. They have either a green or purple-coloured skin with bright red seeds. The entire fig is edible except for the stalk. Eat when ripe - simply wash and eat. They are also served dried and are used in many pickles and chutneys.

- Gooseberry - it is possible to get both sweet and tart gooseberries, with the sweet variety being almost double the size of the tart variety - these often turn golden when ripe, and can be eaten raw, while the tart variety has to be cooked. Enjoyed throughout Europe and the UK since the 1500s, the tart variety is perfect for preserves. Available from late spring to late summer, they are another fruit that it would be a good idea to buy and freeze when in season. Prepare before using by topping and tailing.

- Plum - there are quite a few varieties of plum, ranging from small fruits that can be dark purple or greenish/yellow in colour to bright red. All have stones and most can be eaten raw when ripe or cooked in order to eat.

- Apricot - a type of plum with a soft, furry skin and a kernel which, if cracked, has an almond aroma. It can be eaten raw or cooked and can also be dried, which then enables the apricot to be stored in an airtight container. The dried apricot is used extensively in Middle Eastern dishes.

- Damson - members of the plum family that were cultivated way back in ancient times. The Romans introduced the damson to England. A small, very dark purple fruit, which needs to be very ripe to eat raw. They are used mainly for making jam.

∾ Greengage - a small, greenish/yellow fruit, delicious if eaten completely ripe. Another member of the plum family and becoming increasingly scarce. Grown in France, where they are known as Reine Claude.

∾ Prune - these come from a few different varieties of plum and can now officially be called 'dried plums'. Once dried, they turn black and the flesh becomes chewy. Grown in the US and Europe, they, like the apricot, are used in Middle Eastern dishes. Both the apricot and prunes are very healthy, having good digestive qualities.

∾ Victoria Plum - perhaps the best-known and most delicious of all the larger plums. Grown extensively, both in private gardens and orchards in England, they are used by the home cook in many delicious desserts and preserves. First discovered during Queen Victoria's reign in a garden in Sussex.

∾ Strawberry - these vary in size, taste and texture depending on which variety is grown. They are grown by pick-your-own outlets, which over the years have become very popular, as well as by farmers under glass or in polytunnels, and by the homeowner, who will grow them in strawberry pots, window boxes or small vegetable plots. They are now grown and exported throughout the world. The sweet and juicy flavour of the British strawberry is one of the best, and is at its height at the time of the Wimbledon Tennis Fortnight, when strawberries and cream are a must for all. Strawberries are a seasonal fruit, but are now grown around the world so they are available all year round. Do not contain much pectin, so need additional pectin.

∾ Raspberry - a small, dark red fruit with edible pips. Like the strawberry, they are grown extensively throughout the world. but there are a few weeks when they are not so readily available. The Scottish raspberry, many say, has the best taste and aroma. These appear when the English varieties have finished, normally late summer/early autumn. Raspberries have a medium pectin content, so do need a little more pectin added, often in the form of lemon juice.

❧ Loganberry, Tayberry and Boysenberry - all similar to raspberries, but larger and deeper in colour. They are not normally grown commercially but by specialist or home growers.

❧ Melon - there are quite a few melon varieties readily available, including watermelons, which are the largest. They have a bright, variegated green rind with red flesh and have numerous black seeds, which need to be discarded. They are a very refreshing fruit and can be eaten as a savoury as well as sweet dish. Grown in tropical countries such as the Caribbean as well as in warm parts of America and Europe.

❧ Charentais Melon - has a pale cream, fragrant flesh and a pale green rind with darker green stripes. Due to its fragrant taste and aroma, it is very popular and is eaten both as a sweet and savoury fruit. It is available most of the year and is grown extensively throughout the world. Needs to be eaten ripe and quickly ripens when left in a warm room for 3-4 days. Press the end lightly with a finger to see if it is ripe; it will yield slightly.

❧ Ogen Melon - small melon with a sweet taste and orange-coloured flesh with a pale green rind. First grown commercially on a kibbutz in Israel. Available from spring to midwinter; allow one melon per person.

Ingredients ~ Fruit

- **Honeydew Melon** - perhaps the most popular and best known of all. They have a bright yellow, ridged rind and pale, creamy white to green flesh. When ripe, they are very sweet and juicy. Available all year round in most countries. Can be used as a starter and is often served with Parma ham or as a dessert.

- **Cantaloupe Melon** - has a sweet, fragrant and juicy, pale orange flesh. It is available most of the year and is reputed to have its origins in Asia. Like its counterparts, it can be used for both sweet and savoury purposes.

- **Gallia Melon** - perhaps the next most popular melon after the Honeydew. It has a sweet-tasting, juicy flesh with a pale green rind that turns golden when ripe. It is said that it is a hybrid, a cross between a Honeydew and a Cantaloupe. A melon grower achieved this in Israel in the 1970s. It has a pale green/white, sweet-tasting, juicy flesh with a mottled rind that looks like the bark of a tree. The rind turns from green to golden when ripe. Available most of the year. Again suitable for both sweet and savoury dishes.

- **Mango** - a native to India, this is a large, oval fruit that has a large pit (stone) in the centre. The skin can be dark green or orange/red with a sweet and juicy orange-coloured flesh, which tastes similar to a peach or nectarine. Used in many Indian accompaniments, as well as the famous Mango Chutney. The flesh is also pulped into juices. Available from midwinter to early autumn. It can also be bought in cans.

- **Passion Fruit** - a small, round fruit with a dark, almost black skin, and flesh that is unbelievably aromatic. The flesh contains many seeds. When ripe, the fruit becomes extremely wrinkled. Use by cutting in half, scooping out the pulp and seeds; pass the seeds and pulp through a sieve and use the juice.

The seeds are often used for decoration, but are not good to eat. Said to have originated in Argentina, Brazil and surrounding countries. It is now grown in many hot climates around the world, from New Zealand to Sri Lanka.

∾ Papaya or Pawpaw - native to Central America and available in the spring and summer months. It has a long, oval shape with orange coloured skin. The flesh is slightly sweet and not that juicy, but very soft when ripe, and bruises easily. When cut in half, small, black seeds are revealed which are to be scooped out and discarded. Like the mango, it is also used both in sweet and savoury dishes and juiced as well.

∾ Peach - have been around for more than 2,000 years and originated in China. They have a slightly velvety skin with a fragrant, juicy flesh when ripe and a large stone in the centre, which is discarded. The flesh is either yellow, which is the more common colour, or white. Available in the summer. Some are imported to the UK from warmer climates in the winter months, especially around December. Nectarines are very similar to peaches, except that they have a shiny, smooth skin. Both need warm, sunny climates to grow and both are eaten fresh when ripe or used in desserts or preserves.

∾ Pineapple - a tropical fruit grown in most hot countries. Some countries use the leaves to make textiles. Pineapple is, in fact, a cluster of fruits from the Ananas tree, which come together during growing to form the pineapple. It is native to South America, but is grown in many tropical climates. It is eaten fresh, after discarding the spiky leaves or plume as well as the brown, spiky skin and hard central core. It is also available canned or as juice, crystallised or used in preserves, pickles and chutneys.

∞ Pomegranate - native to Iran, this is one of the oldest fruits known. It is about the size of a medium orange with a waxy skin that is yellow with hints of red. Cutting the fruit in half reveals the many seeds that are enclosed. These are surrounded by a small amount of flesh. The flesh and seeds are often removed and kept whole and added to dishes as decoration, or are sieved and the juice used. Normally eaten raw, although it can be added at the end of cooking. Available midwinter.

∞ Quince - small apple-like fruit native to Asia, which is grown in the UK and other parts of Europe. It is mainly used for preserves and is far too bitter to eat raw.

∞ Rhubarb - there is some debate as to whether rhubarb is a fruit or a vegetable. These days, it is used mainly as a fruit or in preserves. It was grown both by the Chinese and the Ancient Greeks as long ago as 2500 BC and is native to Tibet. There are two main varieties: pink or champagne rhubarb, which is forced under glass to grow early and results in a delicate, long, pale pink stem; or garden rhubarb, which is sturdy with a far thicker stem, pale green, streaked with red. Only the stalk is edible; the large leaves should be discarded as they are poisonous. Available from early spring for only a few weeks. It is grown both for its eating qualities and by the Chinese for medicinal purposes.

∞ Dried Fruits - these are also used in preserves, pickles and chutneys. Raisins, sultanas and currants, all of which come from grapes, as well as apricots and dates, are ideal in chutney and impart a natural sweetness. More exotic dried fruits such as mangoes, cranberries, cherries, dates and figs are ideal for pickles. Dried fruits should be used quickly, otherwise they will soon spoil and become too dry and lose their flavour. Many fruits also start to crystallise if left too long before using. Some fruits are candied, such as pineapple, cherries, papaya and angelica. These are fine to use, but the sugar needs washing off before use.

Ingredients ~ Vegetables

࿔

The condition of the produce used when making chutneys, pickles and preserves is extremely important. Vegetables, like fruit, also need to be sound, free from bruises or damaged pieces. There are a few vegetables that are fine for freezing and using later. This is especially useful in times of glut or when time is short. However, there are some vegetables not recommended for freezing, including green vegetables such as beans, cabbage, broccoli or spinach. It is not recommended to freeze potatoes, onions, garlic or aubergines either. Peppers would be fine, as would cauliflower and carrots. You should buy and freeze the vegetables immediately, then use once thawed. Only keep in the freezer for up to 6 months.

∾ Aubergine - also known as eggplant, this is a native to India but is also grown in other hot countries. The most common variety is large and oval with a shiny, purple skin. However, there are other varieties, which range in colour from purple to white. It is now also possible to buy small, round aubergines. As the aubergines get older, the white flesh becomes bitter and needs slicing and sprinkling with salt, which releases the bitter juices; these slices then need lightly rinsing and patting dry with kitchen paper. The flesh is studded with tiny black seeds and the flesh is not eaten raw.

∾ Avocado Pear - oval-shaped with a stone or pit in the centre. Some say they are a fruit and some a vegetable.

They are generally eaten raw but can be heated. They are native to South America and are now grown in Israel, the Mediterranean and other hot climates. One of the best known is the small purple avocado, which has a rough skin and is called Haas. There is also a larger green avocado with a smooth, shiny skin. Both taste very similar to each other. They should be eaten when ripe, though it is best to buy before they are completely ripe, otherwise they will quickly spoil. Discard the stone and skin before eating.

∾ Bell Pepper - these are extremely popular, so it is extraordinary to think that they only started being imported to the UK in the early 1960s. They come in a variety of colours: red, green, yellow, orange and black. They are also known as sweet peppers and capsicums. Believed to be native to South America, they are now grown worldwide, and play an important part in many cuisines. Unlike its cousin, the chilli pepper, is does not contain hot, spicy properties. However, it is still important that the seeds and membrane are discarded before using in savoury dishes, chutneys and pickles.

∾ Beetroot - closely related to chard and spinach beet, which was developed from a seashore plant in Germany in the Middle Ages. Also related to sugar beet from which sugar is obtained. Now grown extensively in Europe, it is a popular root vegetable that needs cooking before eating. It can be eaten cold, in soup such as borscht, roasted or in salads. It can also be used in chutneys and pickles as well as being preserved in brine.

∾ Carrot - believed to be native to Europe, the Dutch first started cultivating them in the Middle Ages. To begin with, they were black in colour and this was thought to be unattractive for eating purposes, so, over the years, the colour was changed to orange. One of the most important vegetables, they are grown worldwide.

❧ Cauliflower - first cultivated in the Middle East, this came to Europe in the Middle Ages. They are generally cooked before eating and the stalk and leaves are discarded. Some say that adding a little lemon juice to the cooking water helps to preserve the white of the florets. An important vegetable when making piccalilli.

❧ Celery - developed from wild celery in the 16th century by Italian gardeners. An important salad vegetable, it can also be braised in the oven and served with a white sauce. It is also used for flavouring, as it has a very distinctive flavour similar to aniseed. There are two types: one that is predominantly green with both leaves and stalk green; and the other variety where both the leaves and stalk are white. Grown worldwide and available the whole year.

❧ Courgette - a member of the squash family and similar in appearance to a baby marrow. Grown throughout Europe and Asia, they are extremely versatile. Latest developments have produced the baby courgette, a yellow courgette as well as a round variety. The flower is also eaten, dipped in batter and lightly deep-fried.

❧ Garlic - perhaps the most loved or hated ingredient. You either love it or hate it no matter how it is served. This is most probably due to its extremely pungent taste and aroma. It is a member of the lily family and was used as early as the Ancient Egyptians, Greeks and Chinese. It comes as a bulb, with the whole garlic referred to as a bulb, while each segment is a clove. These are normally peeled, then crushed, chopped or sliced. Garlic is grown and used worldwide. A typical dish that uses much garlic is the French 'Chicken with 40 cloves', where, after cooking, the soft garlic pulp is squeezed onto toast and eaten. It is also possible to find smoked and wild garlic.

- **Onion** - used worldwide in all cuisines, this is known by many as the 'King of Vegetables'. There are many varieties available, from yellow to red and white onions. These everyday onions are referred to as the common, bulb or garden onion. They are used in all types of recipes and eaten both raw and cooked. Other onions include baby onions, spring onions and shallots plus the very large Spanish onions that are used for stuffing. Onions have been around for thousands of years and there is evidence that the Ancient Romans, Greeks and Egyptians used onions, as well as the Chinese.

- **Squash** - many different types of squash are grown throughout the world and have been for thousands of years. Varieties include: Butternut, a winter squash with a sweet, nutty taste, yellow skin and orange flesh; and Acorn, a winter variety, shaped, as its name suggests, like an acorn with dark green, ridged skin. New varieties have been developed and include a Golden Acorn and a multicoloured one too. Pattypan or Sunburst squash are small squashes, about 5-7.5 cm/2-3 ins in size, and shaped a little like a flying saucer with scalloped edges round the edge of each. They come in yellow, green and white with variants on these colours. Pumpkins are also members of the squash family.

- **Tomato** - few ingredients have played such a huge role in food as the tomato. Originating in South America, it was first called the 'love apple'. It is also related to the nightshade family and was first thought to be poisonous and used for decoration only. However, it gained popularity for eating and is now used around the world. There are a few varieties, from the large beefsteak, the plum, to the cherry tomato, as well as the Mexican green tomato, called tomallito, which should not be confused with green, unripe tomatoes. It is also the basis of many sauces.

Ingredients ~ Spices and Herbs

℮

Both spices and herbs play an important role when making preserves, chutneys, and pickles. They will impart much of the flavour and need to be added at the correct time. Spices are normally added at the beginning, while herbs are added towards or at the end of the cooking process. The condition of both is also highly critical. If either are old, much of their valuable taste, aroma and perfume will be lost. The way they are stored also plays an important role in preserving.

Spices

Spices should be bought on a regular basis from a reputable source and kept in a cool, dark place and used within 2-3 months. This applies especially to ready-ground spices. Use spices sparingly to begin with, until you are sure about the different flavours and to give your taste buds time to develop.

- Allspice - still grown entirely in its country of origin, the Caribbean. It was discovered by Columbus who was searching for pepper and thought he had found it, and so called it Jamaica pepper. It has a warm fragrance, with a pungent, peppery taste of cloves, cinnamon and nutmeg. Most of the flavour can be found in the shell.

- Cardamom - comes from India and other Asian countries in green and black pods. Both are similar in taste and are highly aromatic. The flavour is in the seeds, which are released when the pods are lightly bashed.

❧ Chilli Powder - there are many different chillies grown in most hot countries. The chilli can vary in heat in the mouth when eating, from 1-10, with 10 being the hottest. A good guide to follow is that the smaller the chilli, the hotter it is. The heat is contained in the oil that is in both the seeds and inside the membrane, to which the seeds are attached. Great care should be taken when first eating and handling fresh chillies. Chillies are often dried, which makes them hotter still - these dried chillies are then ground into powder.

❧ Cinnamon - native to Sri Lanka, this comes both ground and in sticks of varying lengths. If using the sticks, they need to be lightly bashed in order to release their flavour. An aromatic, sweet spice, used for both sweet and savoury dishes.

❧ Cloves - very pungent with a warm, peppery and camphory aroma. Used either whole or ground, the whole spice needs to be lightly pounded to help release the flavour. Only a few are required to flavour a dish or sauce. Native to Indonesia, it became popular in many countries thanks to the Spice Trail.

❧ Coriander - both a herb and a seed, this is used for many dishes throughout the world. Every part of the plant is used, the leaves, stems and root, and each imparts a slightly different taste. This spice is one of the most important in Chinese and Asian dishes. It is possible to buy the seeds, which should be ground in a pestle and mortar just before using for maximum aroma and taste. Ground coriander is used straight from the jar. Ensure that it is dry-fried with the other spices and before other ingredients are added, otherwise there is a danger that the spice will taste raw. If kept too long, the spice could taste musty.

∾ Cumin - together with coriander, this has had a large impact on all Asian dishes. It was originally grown on the banks of the Nile in Ancient Egypt, but is now grown in most hot countries. It has small, long, brown seeds, which are pounded in a pestle and mortar to release their flavour. If preferred, use ground cumin.

∾ Fenugreek - cultivated throughout the world and used extensively in Indian and Middle Eastern dishes. Its name can be translated as Greek hay, but in fact is not featured much in Greek food. Both the leaves and the seeds are used, with the dried leaves smelling similar to hay. It smells like curry powder with celery overtones and a slight bitterness.

∾ Ginger - a very versatile spice that can be used in both sweet and savoury dishes. Asian food uses galangal in place of fresh ginger root; the taste and appearance are very similar. Ginger is warm with a slight hint of pepper. Grown in the East in ancient times, it was used by the Ancient Greeks and Romans, plus all of the Middle and Far East. By the 15th century, the demand in Europe was so great that it started being grown in Italy and other European countries. The ginger root is very aromatic with a fresh, hot and tangy taste with hints of lemon. Asia and the Far East use fresh ginger or galangal more than the dried powder. If fresh ginger is very fresh, it does not need peeling first - simply grate or slice. It is also found crystallised or as stem ginger, both of which are highly popular. Used in both sweet and savoury recipes. A popular sweet is crystallised ginger coated in chocolate.

- **Horseradish** - a perennial plant of the Brassica family, which also includes mustard. It is grown in Europe and the UK and Southeast Asia. It is whitish in colour and is grated before use. It normally has a very strong, peppery taste and is served mixed with cream with smoked mackerel or roast beef.

- **Mace/Nutmeg** - mace is the outer casing of the whole nutmeg and has a very distinctive rich, spicy flavour and aroma. Nutmeg is generally used grated for sweet dishes, while mace is more for savoury dishes and some preserves. Mace is normally left in a liquid such as warm milk to infuse prior to making a sauce such as Béchamel sauce. The whole nutmeg is normally freshly grated into a dish such as rice pudding prior to cooking. Mace comes in small pieces and is referred to as 'a blade of mace', while nutmeg generally comes whole and is grated when required. It can be found ready-ground. It comes from Southeast Asia.

- **Mustard** - bright yellow spice with a hot, peppery taste. There are also black and white mustard, whose seeds are used in many Asian dishes, especially curry. They are dry-fried until the seeds pop, which releases their aroma and taste. The Romans introduced mustard to Britain and it quickly became popular due to it being cheap. Now grown in many countries including the UK.

- **Paprika** - bright red powder used extensively in Hungary and Spain, where it is called Pimentón. It comes from the red bell pepper or red chilli pepper, producing either a mild or a hot paprika.

- **Pepper** - this spice has been around for over 3,000 years and is one of the most important spices ever. It was carried to different countries along the Spice Trail. Pepper is native to Asia and is used worldwide in all cuisines. It grows on a vine and the peppercorns are the sun-dried berries. Pepper is available either as whole peppercorns or ground, and comes in black, white, red, pink and green. Technically, the red, pink and green varieties are not pepper, as they come from a different plant, of which they are the sun-ripened berries. They are preserved whole in brine or vinegar. The outer casing is soft and edible and imparts a delicate, fruity, sweet taste, while the inner part leaves a mild peppery taste when eaten. Green peppercorns have a fresh taste, with a light pungency. All three should be kept in the refrigerator to preserve their aroma and taste.

∞ Saffron - reputed to be the most expensive spice of all, it comes from the dried stigma of a crocus, which is native to the Mediterranean and the Far East. It has the colour of gold when soaked in a little warm water. Beware of imitations, which are far inferior. Has a warm, earthy and penetrating flavour.

∞ Star Anise - used extensively in Asian dishes, it is so called as it is in the shape of a dark brown star. It has a sweet, pungent aroma with tastes of fennel and anise with hints of liquorice. Native to the Far East, especially Vietnam, it was introduced into Europe in the 17th century.

∞ Turmeric - this is often referred to as 'poor mans saffron'. It comes from India and Middle Eastern countries and is used extensively in curries and other spice dishes. It imparts a strong yellow colour to any dish.

Herbs

Herbs impart a freshness to food, which spices cannot. The way that herbs are treated is very important, as, regardless of being either fresh or dried, badly treated herbs will quickly lose aroma and taste. If using dried herbs, as with spices, they need to be bought on a regular basis, as they do not keep for more than a year and need to be kept in a cool, dark place, not in a spice rack in the kitchen with the sun shining on the little bottles or packs. Fresh herbs are best if picked fresh and used immediately. It is very easy to grow your own in a window box, pots in the garden or, if you are lucky, in a herb garden. Herbs are attractive plants and look good even in the smallest garden, growing among the flowers.

Once picked, the herbs should be lightly rinsed and chopped just before use. Most herbs are added at the end of cooking, but the stronger-tasting herbs such as bay leaves, rosemary, thyme or oregano are often added before cooking.

- Basil/Sweet Basil - a very pungent and sweet, spicy herb. It is aromatic and is used extensively in Italian, Greek and Asian dishes. It combines well with tomatoes and is the main ingredient of pesto. Basil has been cultivated for more than 5,000 years and is thought to have originated from Asian countries such as Cambodia, Vietnam and Laos. It has either a bright green or purple leaf and stalk. It is very easy to grow, even on a windowsill and is now available in growing pots all year round.

- Bay Leaf - fresh or dried bay leaves are used to flavour many dishes and are normally added at the beginning of cooking. Ideal for flavouring soups and casseroles. The bay grows into a tree if left to grow wild and is related to the laurel. Bay leaves develop their strong, distinctive aroma and flavour a few weeks after picking and drying. There are many varieties grown throughout the world, as far afield as California and Indonesia. Bay leaves have been around for thousands of years.

❧ Coriander - also known as cilantro in many countries such as the US, or Chinese parsley in the Orient, this is used in many different cuisines and has been around since ancient times. It is a very aromatic herb, with the stalks and the root used (wash well before using) as well as the leaf. It is one of the main herbs in Asian cuisines and plays an important part in curry dishes.

❧ Mint - there are many varieties of mint, from spearmint to peppermint and apple mint, with many hybrids available. Spearmint is the everyday mint that is normally grown in most gardens and used by many. Mint has been around for over 5,000 years and is popular in Southern and Northern Europe as well as in Africa, the Middle East, Asia, Australia and the US. Having a highly pungent aroma, mint suits all types of dishes from savoury to sweet, while in drinks it is easy to see why it is so popular.

❧ Oregano/ Wild Marjoram - a warm and aromatic herb with slight, spicy, bitter overtones, which have been known to numb the tongue. Used in Europe, especially Greece and Italy, it complements many of their favourite ingredients, such as tomatoes, cheese and aubergines. It has also been used for many years in Asia. The best oregano is grown in warm, dry conditions such as the Greek mountains, while the name is a derivation of the Greek word for 'mountain'. The Ancient Greeks and Romans used the herb as a poultice for aching joints and in some areas this continues even today. Marjoram is closely related to oregano but lacks the medicinal properties and has a less spicy taste – and does not numb the mouth!

∾ Rosemary - native to the Mediterranean, this is related to the mint family. It is a woody plant with long, spiky leaves and white, pink or blue flowers. It is a very robust plant and survives well on sea dunes and in other dry, arid areas. It has been around since ancient times. It grows wild in many countries, including the US. It is used both for flavouring, as it has a robust, camphory aroma, and for decoration purposes. It is not recommended to eat it raw.

∾ Sage - a popular herb that has been around for thousands of years, not only in the Mediterranean but in many other parts of the world. It has elongated, furry leaves that come in a variety of green/grey and purple colours. Having a robust and aromatic flavour, it combines with many foods, especially pork and duck. It was also used in ancient times for medicinal purposes. It is not usually eaten raw.

∾ Thyme - this was around in Ancient Egypt, Rome and Greece and played an important part in the treatment of the body. Not only was thyme used in cooking, it was also very important for embalming the dead, adding to the bath, burning as incense and as a room purifier. In the Middle Ages, it was also used to induce sleep and to make warriors courageous. Nowadays, it is used worldwide for flavouring. There are many varieties, all of which combine well with food. Especially fragrant is the lemon-scented variety.

Setting Agents, Sugars & Vinegars

Setting Agents

Jams, jellies and marmalades will only set if they have the correct amount of a setting agent and sugar. The setting agent is pectin - either natural or commercial.

- Commercial pectin is made from apples and comes in liquid form. It is generally added after boiling and is normally used for fruits that have a low natural pectin level, such as strawberries. It is also used for preserves where the fruit is only lightly boiled so as to retain larger pieces of fruit, as in raspberry jam.

- Fruits with a high pectin content include black- and redcurrants, cooking apples, crab apples, cranberries, damsons, gooseberries, lemons, limes, Seville oranges and quinces.

- Fruits with a medium pectin content include dessert apples, apricots, blueberries, blackberries, greengages, loganberries, plums and raspberries.

- Fruits with a low pectin content include banana, cherries, figs, grapes, melons, peaches, nectarines, pineapple, rhubarb and strawberries.

- Lemon and lime juices contain a high level of pectin and can be added to the pan with the fruit to help with the set. Citric acid can also be used. It is important that the correct amount of pectin and sugar are used in order to obtain a good set.

Sugar

In the UK, we have sugars that have been specifically produced for preserves: these are preserving sugar and jam sugar.

- Preserving sugar should be used with fruits that have a high pectin content. The large sugar crystals allow the water to move freely between them on the base of the pan, which will reduce burning and create less froth and scum.

- Jam sugar has a balanced amount of natural pectin and citric acid, which helps fruits with a low pectin content to set.

- Light muscovado or dark muscovado sugar is often used in chutneys and pickle-making. It is unrefined and has a strong molasses taste.

Vinegar and Other Ingredients

Vinegar is a preserving agent and is the most important part of any pickle or chutney. Use the best quality available.

- Distilled or white vinegar is best used for preserves where a lighter colour is required.

- Malt vinegar gives a darker colour and a more intense flavour.

- Table or cooking salt is used to make a brine to soak vegetables or fruits used for pickles. You must rinse off the brine thoroughly before use.

- Brandy, rum, whiskey or Cointreau are added to sugar syrup to preserve fruit.

Classic Jams

Preserves

Traditional jams and preserves are delicious accompaniments to savoury and sweet dishes and snacks. Classic Strawberry Jam is ideal for your morning toast and Summer Berry Conserve is perfect for spreading on croissants. There are also recipes here for all occasions: Pear and Cinnamon Jam for a Christmassy taste or exotic Apricot and Passion Fruit Jam for an elegant tea party.

Classic Strawberry Jam

Ɛ

Fills about 5 x 450 g/ 1 lb jars

1.5 kg/3 lb ripe, unblemished whole strawberries
50 ml/2 fl oz freshly squeezed lemon juice, strained
1.5 kg/3 lb jam sugar
1 tsp butter

Cook's Tip

When choosing strawberries for jam-making, do not be tempted to choose cheaper berries. Berries that are for sale at a cheap price are not the bargain they appear to be. Probably they are overripe or damaged and if used for jam or jelly-making will give a poor result as both the taste and keeping qualities could be affected.

Hull and rinse the strawberries and place in a preserving pan with the lemon juice. Place over a gentle heat and simmer for 15-20 minutes, stirring occasionally, until the fruit has collapsed and is really soft.

Add the sugar and heat, stirring occasionally, until the sugar has dissolved. Add the butter, then bring to the boil and boil rapidly for 10-20 minutes until setting point is reached.

Allow to cool for 8-10 minutes, skim, then pot into warm sterilised jars. Cover the surface with waxed discs and, when cold, cover and label.

Simple Raspberry Jam

Fills about 5 x 450 g/ 1 lb jars

1.8 kg/4 lb ripe, unblemished
whole raspberries
50 ml/2 fl oz freshly squeezed
lemon juice, strained
1.8 kg/4 lb jam sugar
1 tsp butter

Flavour Tip

Other flavours can be added if
liked. Replace 450 g/1 lb of
the raspberries with
loganberries or tayberries if
available, or add 2 lightly
bruised lemongrass stalks and
4 lightly bruised green
cardamom pods to the fruit
when starting to cook.
Remember to discard the
spices before potting.

Hull and lightly rinse the raspberries and
place in a preserving pan with the lemon
juice. Place over a gentle heat and simmer for
15-20 minutes, stirring occasionally, until
the fruit has collapsed and is really soft.

Add the sugar and heat, stirring occasionally,
until the sugar has dissolved. Add the butter,
then bring to the boil and boil rapidly for
10-20 minutes until setting point is reached.
Remember to skim off any scum that might rise
to the surface, using a slotted spoon.

Allow to cool for 8-10 minutes, skim, then
pot into warm sterilised jars. Cover the
surface with waxed discs and, when cold,
cover and label.

Blackcurrant Conserve

Fills 10 x 450 g/1 lb jars

1.8 kg/4 lb ripe, ripe
blackcurrants
1.7 litres/3 pints water
2.75 kg/6 lb jam sugar
1 tsp butter

Using the prongs of a fork, strip the blackcurrants off their stalks and lightly rinse. Place the fruit into a preserving pan and add the water. Place over a gentle heat and simmer for 20-30 minutes until the blackcurrants have collapsed completely and their skins are very soft. It is important that the fruit is cooked until the skins are soft, otherwise they will remain tough, which will affect the finished jam. Stir occasionally during the cooking process.

Once the blackcurrants are really soft, add the sugar and heat, stirring occasionally, until the sugar has dissolved. Add the butter, then bring to the boil and boil rapidly for 10-20 minutes until setting point is reached. Remember to skim off any scum that might rise to the surface, using a slotted spoon.

Allow to cool for 8-10 minutes, skim, then pot into warm sterilised jars. Cover the surface with waxed discs and, when cold, cover and label.

Cook's Tip

Use a mixture of currants.

Speedy Apricot Jam

Fills about 6 x 450 g/ 1 lb jars

1.8 kg/4 lbs ripe apricots
150 ml/¼ pint freshly squeezed lemon juice
250 ml/8 fl oz water
1.75 kg/4 lbs jam sugar
50 g/2 oz ready-to-eat dried apricots
25 g/1 oz flaked almonds

Cook's Tip

The kernels from the stones can be added if liked. Crack open a few stones, remove the kernels and blanch before adding to the pan with the fruit.

Lightly rinse the apricots, discarding any stalks. Chop the apricots and discard the stones and place in a microwave-proof bowl. Add the lemon juice and water, cover and cook on high for 5-6 minutes until the apricots are very soft. Remove and pour into a preserving pan.

Place the preserving pan on the hob over a medium heat and stir in the sugar. Cook gently, stirring occasionally, until the sugar has completely dissolved.

Meanwhile, finely chop the dried apricots, then add to the pan and bring to the boil. Boil for 15 minutes, or until setting point is reached. Remove from the heat and allow to stand for 5 minutes. Stir in the flaked almonds. Pot, cover and label in the usual way.

Black Cherry Jam with Kirsch

**Fills about 5 x 450 g/
1 lb jars**

1.75 kg/4 lb dark cherries
such as Morello
125 ml/4 fl oz freshly squeezed
lemon or orange juice,
strained
1.25 kg/2½ lb granulated sugar
1 tsp butter
4 tbsp Kirsch or to taste
250 ml/8 fl oz liquid pectin

Lightly rinse the cherries, then discard any stalks and stones. Place in a large preserving pan with a lid and add the strained lemon or orange juice. Place over a gentle heat and bring to the boil. Cover with the lid and simmer gently for 20 minutes, or until the cherries have collapsed and are very soft.

Add the sugar and heat, stirring, until the sugar has completely dissolved, then add the butter and kirsch. Bring to the boil and boil rapidly for 3 minutes. Remove from the heat and stir in the pectin. Cool for 10 minutes, then pot and cover in the usual way.

Cook's Tip

If your preserving pan does not have a lid, use a large ordinary pan and transfer the cooked cherries to the preserving pan afterwards.

Delicious Plum Jam

❦

Fills 5 x 450 g/1 lb jars

1.5 kg/3 lb ripe but firm plums
450 ml/$^3/_4$ pint water
1.5 kg/3 lb preserving sugar
1 tsp butter

Cook's Tip

Add some spices to give a
spicy new flavour, such as 6
lightly cracked cardamom pods
or 2-3 lightly bruised
lemongrass stalks.

Fruit Tip

Other stoned fruits can be
used if liked, such as
greengages, damsons,
peaches or nectarines.

Rinse the plums, discarding any damaged
fruits, cut in half and remove the stones.
Crack a few of the stones open and remove
the kernels and reserve them.

Place the plums, reserved kernels and water
in a preserving pan, bring to the boil
and simmer for 40 minutes, or until the
plums are soft and pulpy. Add the sugar,
heat gently, stirring until the sugar has
dissolved, then add the butter.

Bring to the boil and boil rapidly for
10-15 minutes until setting point is
reached. Cool for 8 minutes, then pot and
cover in warm sterilised jars. Cover the
jam with a small waxed disc and, when cold,
cover, label and store in a cool cupboard.

Apricot ❧ Passion Fruit Jam

Makes about 5 x 450 g/ 1 lb jars

900 g/2 lb ripe, firm apricots
3 ripe passion fruits
150 ml/$\frac{1}{4}$ pint freshly squeezed lemon juice
900 g/2 lb preserving sugar
1 tsp butter

Make a small cross at the stalk end of each apricot and place in a large, heatproof bowl. Cover with boiling water and leave for 2-3 minutes until the skins are beginning to peel away. Drain and, when cool enough to handle, peel. Cut the apricots in half and discard the stones. Place the fruit in a preserving pan. Scoop out the pulp and seeds from the passion fruits and add to the apricots.

Add all the lemon juice and sugar and place over a gentle heat and simmer for 30 minutes, or until the fruit is soft and pulpy. Add the butter and stir until melted.

Bring to the boil and boil rapidly for 15 minutes, or until setting point is reached. Cool for 10-15 minutes before potting into warm sterilised jars; cover with a waxed disc. Once cold, cover and label.

Cook's Tip

Passion fruits are ripe and ready to use when very wrinkled. If liked, sieve the pulp to discard the seeds.

Blackberry   Apple Jam

Fills about 8 x 450 g/ 1 lb jars

1.8 kg/4 lb ripe blackberries
300 ml/1/2 pint water
700 g/11/2 lb cooking apples
(peeled weight)
2.75 kg/6 lb preserving sugar

Remove and discard any remaining hulls from the blackberries and wash well. Place in a heavy-based saucepan and add half the water. Place over a gentle heat and bring to the boil. Simmer gently, stirring occasionally, for 10-15 minutes until the blackberries are soft. Remove and reserve while cooking the apples.

Peel the apples, discarding the core and then chop. Place in a preserving pan with the remaining water and place over a gentle heat. Simmer for 12-15 minutes, stirring occasionally with a wooden spoon, until the apples are soft and pulpy. Mash with a spoon or potato masher until a pulp is formed with no large lumps.

Add the blackberries to the apple pulp, then stir in the sugar. Place over a gentle heat and cook for 10 minutes, or until the sugar has dissolved. Bring to the boil and boil rapidly until setting point is reached.

Allow to cool for at least 5 minutes before potting and label in the usual way.

Cook's Tip

Wild brambles can also be used if liked.

Marrow 🐝 Ginger Jam

Fills about 6 x 450 g/ 1 lb jars

1 large marrow, about 1.8 kg/4 lb (peeled and seeded weight)
1.8 kg/4 lb granulated sugar
50 g/2 oz root ginger
thinly peeled zest and juice of 2 large lemons

Peel the marrow, discarding the seeds and cut the flesh into small pieces. Place in a large bowl and sprinkle with 450 g/1 lb of the sugar. Cover and leave overnight.

Next day, bruise the root ginger with a mallet or rolling pin to release the flavour and reserve. Place the marrow with the liquid that has been extracted overnight into a preserving pan.

Cut a small square of muslin, then place the bruised root ginger with the lemon zest onto the muslin and tie up to contain. Add to the marrow together with the lemon juice.

Simmer for 30 minutes, or until very soft, then add the remaining sugar and heat until dissolved, stirring occasionally. When the sugar has dissolved, bring to the boil and boil gently until setting point is reached and the marrow looks transparent. Cool for 10 minutes, then pot and cover in the usual way.

Cook's Tip

Stir in 50 g/2 oz chopped stem ginger before potting.

Rhubarb ❧ Strawberry Jam

Fills about 6 x 450 g/
1 lb jars

700 g/1¹/₂ lb fresh rhubarb
3 tbsp lemon juice
1.5 kg/3 lb preserving sugar
1.2 litres/2 pints water
900 g/2 lb strawberries, hulled
and lightly rinsed
50 g/2 oz piece root ginger,
washed and grated

Trim the rhubarb, wash and cut into short
lengths. Place layers of rhubarb and 450 g/1 lb
of the sugar in a large bowl. Sprinkle with the
lemon juice, cover and leave overnight.

Next day, place the rhubarb and extracted
liquid into a preserving pan and add the water,
strawberries and ginger. Place over a medium
heat and bring to the boil. Reduce the heat
to a simmer and cook gently for 30 minutes,
or until soft and pulpy.

Stir in the remaining sugar and heat gently,
stirring frequently, until the sugar has
dissolved. Bring to the boil and boil rapidly
for 15-20 minutes until setting point is
reached. Cool slightly and skim if necessary.
Pot and cover in the usual way.

Cook's Tip

If liked, add some crystallised
ginger to the jam once setting
point has been reached. Do not
forget to stir before potting.

Blueberry Conserve

Fills 4 x 350 g/
12 oz jars

700 g/1^{1}/$_{2}$ lb blueberries
250 ml/8 fl oz freshly squeezed
orange juice
thinly pared zest of
1 medium orange
1 bruised cinnamon stick, broken
into short lengths
500 g/1 lb 1 oz granulated sugar
175 ml/6 fl oz liquid pectin

Thoroughly rinse the blueberries, discarding
any fruits that are damaged and any stalks.
Place in a preserving pan with the orange
juice. Tie the pared orange zest and
cinnamon stick pieces in a small piece of
muslin and add to the pan. Place the pan
over a gentle heat and simmer for 20
minutes, or until really soft.

Add the sugar and cook gently, stirring
occasionally, until the sugar has completely
dissolved. Bring to the boil and boil for
3 minutes, then draw off the heat and
stir in the pectin. Cool slightly; discard
the spices, then pot and label in the
usual way.

Cook's Tip

A conserve is where the jam
consists of whole fruit. It is
simmered gently in order to
keep the fruit whole. It can be
tricky to get a set, hence the
use of liquid pectin.

Blueberry ❧ Apple Jam

Thoroughly rinse the blueberries, discarding any fruits that are damaged and any stalks. Place in a preserving pan. Peel the cooking apples and discard the cores.

Makes 4 x 350 g/ 12 oz jars

700 g/1 lb 8 oz blueberries
450 g/1 lb cooking apples
250 ml/8 fl oz freshly squeezed orange juice
2 tsp ground cinnamon
1 tsp ground allspice
500 g/1 lb 1 oz granulated sugar
175 ml/6 fl oz liquid pectin

Chop the apples into small pieces, then add to the blueberries together with the orange juice. Sprinkle in the spices. Place the pan over a gentle heat and simmer for 20 minutes, or until really soft.

Add the sugar and cook gently, stirring occasionally, until the sugar has completely dissolved. Bring to the boil and boil for 3 minutes, then draw off the heat and stir in the pectin. Cool slightly, discard the spices, then pot and label in the usual way.

Cook's Tip

Try using a vanilla pod split open, or 1 large cinnamon stick that has been slightly bruised, or 3 whole star anise. If liked, add 1 eating apple, peeled, cored and finely chopped, to the jam after the sugar has dissolved.

Strawberry Conserve

❦

Fills about 5 x 450 g/ 1 lb jars

1.8 kg/4 lb whole strawberries
1.8 kg/4 lb jam sugar

Try to choose strawberries that are of a consistent size. Choose small, ripe strawberries that are free from bruising and any other damage. Hull the berries, then rinse lightly, patting them dry with absorbent kitchen paper.

Choose a large, grease-free bowl and scald by carefully pouring in a kettle of boiling water. Leave for 2-3 minutes, then pour the water away.

Layer the prepared strawberries with the sugar in the clean bowl. Cover with a clean tea towel and leave for 24 hours.

Pour the strawberries and liquid into a preserving pan and heat gently, stirring frequently, until the sugar has dissolved. Bring to the boil and boil rapidly for 5 minutes.

Cook's Tip

This gives a light set, so, once opened, store in the refrigerator.

Meanwhile, wash and scald the bowl again, then pour in the strawberries. Cover with a clean tea towel and leave for 48 hours. Return the strawberries to the preserving pan and bring to the boil, then boil rapidly until setting point is reached. Cool, then pot and label in the usual way.

Reduced-sugar Strawberry Jam

**Fills 3-4 x 450 g/
1 lb jars**

1.5 kg/3 lb ripe strawberries
150 ml/¼ pint freshly squeezed
lemon or lime juice
thinly pared zest of 1 large
lemon or 2 limes
225 g/8 oz jam sugar
225 ml/8 fl oz liquid pectin

Thoroughly rinse the strawberries, discarding any fruits that are damaged and discard any stalks. Place in a preserving pan with the lemon or lime juice. Tie the pared lemon or lime zest in a small piece of muslin and add to the pan. Place the pan over a gentle heat and simmer for 20 minutes, or until really soft.

Add the sugar and cook gently, stirring occasionally, until the sugar has completely dissolved. Bring to the boil and boil for 3 minutes, then draw off the heat and stir in the pectin. Cool slightly; discard the lemon or lime zest. Pot and label in the usual way.

Cook's Tip

Other fruits can be used to make jam with a reduced sugar content. Choose fruits that are naturally sweet, such as raspberries, peaches, apricots and ripe plums, such as Victoria plums.

Summer Berry Conserve

Fills about 5 x 450 g/ 1 lb jars

1.8 kg/4 lb mixed summer berries, such as whole strawberries, raspberries, loganberries, blueberries or blackberries
1.8 kg/4 lb jam sugar
2 tbsp finely grated orange zest

Try to choose berries that are of a consistent size. Choose small, ripe fruits that are free from bruising and any other damage. Hull the berries if necessary, then rinse lightly, patting them dry with absorbent kitchen paper.

Scald a large, heatproof bowl, then layer the prepared berries with the sugar and orange zest in the clean bowl. Cover with a clean tea towel and leave for 24 hours.

Pour the fruit and liquid into a preserving pan and heat gently, stirring frequently, until the sugar has dissolved. Bring to the boil and boil rapidly for 5 minutes.

Meanwhile, wash and scald the bowl again, then pour in the cooked fruit. Cover with a clean tea towel and leave for 48 hours.

Cook's Tip

This gives a light set, so, once opened, store in the refrigerator.

Return the berries to the preserving pan and bring to the boil, then boil rapidly until setting point is reached. Cool, then pot and label in the usual way.

Mango ❧ Cardamom Jam

Fills 3 x 350 g/ 12 oz jars

4 green cardamom pods
1 kg/2 lb ripe mango (450 g/1 lb peeled, stone removed weight)
225 g/8 oz jam sugar
4 tbsp lemon juice, strained
1 tsp butter

Crack open the cardamom pods and reserve. Peel the mango, discard the stone, then chop into small pieces. Place in a mixing bowl. Sprinkle with the cardamom and the sugar, then pour in the lemon juice. Cover and place in a cool place and leave overnight to allow the juices to flow from the mangoes.

Next day, spoon the fruit and juice into a preserving pan or nonreactive saucepan. Place over a medium heat and cook for 10 minutes, stirring frequently to ensure that all the sugar has dissolved. Add the butter.

Bring to a rapid boil, stirring occasionally to ensure that the mango does not stick to the base of the pan. Test for the setting point when the consistency looks thick. Pot and cover immediately with waxed discs and leave until cold before covering with a screw-top lid or cellophane and rubber band.

Cook's Tip

Once setting point is reached, remove from the heat and allow to cool for about 10 minutes before pouring into the warm sterilised jars.

Greengage Conserve

Fills about 6 x 450 g/ 1 lb jars

1.5 kg/3 lb ripe greengages
600 ml/1 pint orange juice
1.5 kg/3 lb jam sugar
1 tsp butter

Choose firm but ripe greengages; discard any bruised or damaged fruit. Cut in half and discard the stones, then rinse lightly. Place the fruit into a preserving pan and add the orange juice.

Place over a gentle heat and simmer for 40 minutes, or until the greengages have collapsed completely and their skins are very soft. Stir frequently, taking care that the fruit does not dry out.

Once the fruit is really soft, add the sugar and heat, stirring occasionally, until the sugar has dissolved. Add the butter, then bring to the boil and boil rapidly for 15-20 minutes until setting point is reached. Remember to skim off any scum that might rise to the surface, using a slotted spoon.

Cook's Tip

It is important that the fruit is cooked until the skins are soft, otherwise the skins will remain tough, which will affect the finished conserve.

Allow to cool for 8-10 minutes, skim, then pot into warm sterilised jars. Cover the surface with waxed discs and, when cold, cover and label.

Delicious Quince Jam

**Fills about 5 x 450 g/
1 lb jars**

1 ripe medium-sized orange,
preferably organic
1.8 kg/4 lb quince
4 tbsp lemon juice, strained
2.25 litres/4 pints water
1.5 kg/3 lb preserving sugar

Cook's Tip

Grate the quince on the larger
holes of a cheese grater.

Scrub the skin of the orange and dry thoroughly,
then remove the zest with a vegetable peeler.
Squeeze out the juice. Reserve.

Wash the quince thoroughly, cut in half and
grate. Make sure you do not grate the core,
which is discarded.

Place the grated quince into a preserving pan or
a large nonreactive saucepan with a lid. Add the
thinly pared orange zest and juice, plus the
lemon juice, together with half the water.

Bring to the boil, stirring occasionally. Reduce
the heat to a simmer, then cover with the lid.
Cook for 20 minutes, or until the quince is tender.

Stir in the remaining water and sugar; cook
gently until the sugar has dissolved. Return
to the boil, then reduce the heat to a simmer.
Cook for a further 30-40 minutes until the
mixture has thickened.

Remove from the heat and cool for 10 minutes
before potting and labelling in the usual manner.

Tangy Gooseberry Jam

Fills about 5 x 450 g/
1 lb jars

1.5 kg/3 lb gooseberries
50 g/2 oz piece root
ginger, grated
900 ml/1^{1}/$_{2}$ pints water
1.5 kg/3 lb preserving sugar

Choose slightly underripe gooseberries. Top and tail them using a pair of scissors. Wash thoroughly and drain in a colander.

Place the gooseberries with the ginger into a preserving pan together with the water. Bring to the boil, then reduce the heat to a gentle simmer. Stir the gooseberries occasionally to ensure that the fruit is not sticking to the pan base. Cook for 35-40 minutes until the fruit is soft.

Drawn the pan off the heat and mash with a potato masher to form a pulp. Stir in the sugar, then return to a gentle simmer, stirring frequently until the sugar has dissolved.

Bring the fruit to a full rolling boil and cook until setting point is reached. Draw off the heat and cool for at least 5 minutes. Place the warm sterilised jars on a wooden board and, using a funnel, fill the jars and cover with a waxed disc. Once cold, cover and label.

Cook's Tip

If the ginger is very fresh, grate on the coarse side of the grater and do not peel.

Pear ✿ Cinnamon Jam

Fills about 5 x 450 g/
1 lb jars

2 kg/4^{1}/$_{2}$ lb pears
3 tbsp lemon juice
1 medium orange
4 tbsp freshly squeezed
orange juice
2 cinnamon sticks or 2 tsp
ground cinnamon
1 litre/1^{3}/$_{4}$ pints water
1.2 kg/2^{1}/$_{2}$ lb jam sugar
1 tsp butter

Cook's Tip

Choose pears that are not
too ripe; slightly hard would
be good.

Peel the pears, discarding the cores, skin
and any bruised parts. Chop into small pieces;
place in a large bowl with lemon juice.
Completely cover with cold water.

Scrub the orange and dry, remove the zest and
squeeze out the juice, adding more juice if
necessary. Reserve. Lightly bash the cinnamon
sticks if using, then place in a small
muslin bag.

Drain the pears and rinse. Place in a preserving
pan with the reserved orange zest, juice and
cinnamon sticks, and the water.

Heat gently and simmer for 20 minutes, or
until the pears are really soft. Add the sugar
and cook gently, stirring frequently, until
the sugar has thoroughly dissolved.

Bring to the boil, then boil steadily for
10-15 minutes until setting point is reached.
Draw off the heat. Discard the cinnamon
sticks, then stir in the butter. Cool before
potting in the usual way.

Spicy Peach Jam

Makes about 6 x 400 g/
14 oz jars

900 g/2 lb ripe, firm peaches
4 whole star anise
150 ml/¹/₄ pint freshly squeezed
lemon juice
900 g/2 lb preserving sugar

Make a small cross at the stalk end of each peach and place in a large bowl. Cover with boiling water and leave for 2-3 minutes, drain and, when cool enough to handle, peel. Cut the peaches in half and discard the stones. Place the fruit in a preserving pan.

Cut out a small piece of muslin and place the star anise in the centre. Tie up with a long piece of string. Tie to the handle of the preserving pan so that the muslin bag sits in the peaches.

Add all the lemon juice and sugar, place over a gentle heat and simmer for 30 minutes, or until the fruit is soft and pulpy.

Bring to the boil and boil rapidly for 15 minutes, or until setting point is reached. Cool for 10-15 minutes before potting into warm sterilised jars, cover with a waxed disc. Once cold, cover and label.

Cook's Tip

Nectarines or apricots could be used in place of the peaches.

Old-fashioned

Jellies

Jellies use the juice from boiled fruits, spices and herbs to create a fresh flavour with a clear, jelly-like consistency. Redcurrant Jelly is a deliciously sweet and fruity spread, while Mint Jelly is a great accompaniment to savoury dishes. You will quickly become familiar with using the 'jelly-bag' to strain out the fruit pulp and may even begin experimenting with the recipes here.

Apple ✺ Chilli Jelly

Fills about 3 x 225 g/ 8 oz jars

8 bell peppers
2 Bramley cooking apples
4-6 red chillies
150 ml/^{1}/$_4$ pint white wine vinegar
1.25 litres/2^1/$_2$ pints water
1 tbsp coriander seeds, lightly crushed
5 cm/2 in piece root ginger, washed and grated
allow 450 g/1 lb preserving sugar for every 600 ml/1 pint extracted juice
250 ml/8 fl oz liquid pectin

Discard the seeds from the peppers, then roughly chop. Wash the apples, discard any bruised or damaged pieces, and roughly chop. Cut 3 chillies in half, discard the seeds and chop. Place them all in a preserving pan with the vinegar, water, coriander seeds and ginger. Bring to the boil and simmer for 1 hour, or until the peppers are really tender. Strain through a jelly bag.

Measure the extract and return to the rinsed preserving pan together with the sugar. Discard the seeds from 1-2 of the remaining chillies, then chop and reserve.

Heat gently, stirring frequently, until the sugar has dissolved. Bring to the boil and boil rapidly for 3 minutes. Draw off the heat; cool for 5 minutes. Skim, then stir in the pectin and chopped chillies. Pot and label in the usual way.

Cook's Tip

Use all the chillies if a very hot jelly is preferred.

Redcurrant Jelly

**Fills about 6 x 225 g/
8 oz jars**

1.8 kg/4 lb redcurrants
1.1 litres/2 pints water
allow 450 g/1 lb preserving
sugar for every 600 ml/1 pint
extracted juice

Wash the redcurrants, removing any leaves or damaged fruit. Place with the water in a large, nonreactive saucepan with a lid and bring to the boil. Reduce the heat to a simmer and cover with the lid. Cook gently for 30-40 minutes, stirring occasionally with a wooden spoon, until the fruit has collapsed.

Remove from the heat, cool slightly, then carefully pour into the scalded jelly bag. Cover with a clean tea towel and leave in a draught-free place to drip through. Do not stir or squeeze the bag, otherwise the jelly may be cloudy.

When all the juice has dripped through, measure the amount extracted and add the sugar.

Place over a gentle heat and cook until the sugar has dissolved. Bring to a rapid boil and boil for 10-15 minutes until setting point is reached. Draw off the heat and cool before pouring into warm sterilised jars and covering with a waxed disc. When cold, secure with a lid and label.

Cook's Tip

Try using black- and redcurrants
for a slightly sweeter jelly.

Thick Damson Jelly

Fills about 4 x 450 g/
1 lb jars

1.8 kg/4 lb ripe damsons
150 ml/¼ pint lemon juice
1 litre/1¾ pints water
allow 450 g/1 lb preserving
sugar for every 600 ml/1 pint
extracted juice

Wash the damsons, discarding any that are badly damaged or bad. Remove the stalks and cut in half. Place in a nonreactive saucepan with a lid. Add the lemon juice and water. Bring to the boil, then the reduce heat to a simmer; cover with the lid. Cook for 40 minutes, or until the damsons are soft. Cool for 5 minutes.

When the damsons have cooled a little, pour into the jelly bag so that the juice will drip into the bowl. Leave in a cool, draught-free place and cover the top with a clean tea towel.

When the juice has dripped through, measure it and pour into a preserving pan. Add the sugar.

Gently heat, stirring until the sugar has dissolved. Bring to a rapid boil and boil for 10-15 minutes until the setting point is reached. Draw off the heat and cool before pouring into warm sterilised jars and covering with a waxed disc. When cold, secure with a lid and label.

Cook's Tip

Make sure that the damsons are ripe for a good flavour.

Apple ❧ Rosemary Jelly

Fills about 3 x 225 g/ 8 oz jars

700 g/1½ lb Bramley cooking apples
1.1 litres/2 pints water
2-3 sprigs fresh rosemary, plus extra for potting
allow 450 g/1 lb preserving sugar per 600 ml/1 pint liquid

Wash the apples and discard the stalks (do not peel or core). Chop, then place in a preserving pan with the water and 2-3 rosemary sprigs. Bring to the boil and simmer for 1 hour, or until the apples are very soft.

Cool slightly before straining through a jelly bag. Once all the juice has been extracted, measure and pour into the preserving pan and add the sugar.

Place over a gentle heat and cook, stirring frequently, until the sugar has completely dissolved. Bring to the boil and boil rapidly for 10-15 minutes until setting point is reached. Remove and cool for at least 5 minutes.

Skim if necessary, then pot. Add 1-2 small sprigs of fresh rosemary, then cover and label in the usual way.

Cook's Tip

Replace the rosemary with a few sprigs of fresh oregano or thyme.

Fresh Mint Jelly

Fills about 6 x 225 g/
8 oz jars

2.25 kg/5 lb Bramley cooking
apples (450 g/1 lb in weight)
1.3 litres/2$\frac{1}{4}$ pints water
bunch fresh mint, plus 2 tbsp
freshly chopped mint
1.5 litres/2$\frac{1}{2}$ pints vinegar
allow 450 g/1 lb preserving
sugar per 600 ml/1 pint liquid
green food colouring (optional)

Wash the apples and chop (do not peel or core), add to the preserving pan with the water and mint. Bring to the boil; simmer for 1 hour. Add the vinegar and boil for 5 minutes.

Cool slightly before straining through a jelly bag. Once all the juice has been extracted, measure and pour into the preserving pan. Add the sugar.

Place over a gentle heat and cook, stirring frequently, until the sugar has completely dissolved. Add a few drops of green food colouring if using. Bring to the boil and boil rapidly for 10-15 minutes until setting point is reached. Remove and cool for at least 5 minutes.

Skim if necessary, then stir in the chopped mint. Pot, cover and label in the usual way.

Cook's Tip

Use mint that has a good strong flavour and make sure it is well washed before using.

Red Wine Jelly (*Confit du Vin*)

Fills about 4 x 175 g/ 6 oz jars

450 g/1 lb cooking apples
600 ml/1 pint water
1 bottle red wine, such as Claret
allow 450 g/1 lb preserving sugar per 600 ml/1 pint liquid

Wash the apples, discarding any damaged or bruised pieces and cut into chunks. (Do not peel or core). Place the chopped apples and cores into a nonreactive saucepan with a lid, together with the water and wine. Bring to the boil, then reduce the heat and simmer for 30 minutes, or until the apples are very soft and pulpy. Pass through a jelly bag.

Measure the juice extracted and pour into the cleaned saucepan or a preserving pan with the sugar. Heat gently, stirring frequently until the sugar has dissolved, then bring to the boil and boil rapidly for 15 minutes, or until the setting point is reached. Cool slightly; skim, then pot and label in the usual way.

Cook's Tips

Other wines, such as white or rosé, can be used in the same way. This jelly is super stirred into meat and chicken casseroles or into gravies.

Autumn Bramble Jelly

℮

Fills about 4 x 225 g/ 8 oz jars

1.8 kg/4 lb just-ripe blackberries
4 tbsp lemon juice
1 litre/3/4 pint water
allow 450 g/1 lb preserving sugar for every 600 ml/1 pint extracted juice
2-3 tbsp crème de cassis (optional)

Wash the blackberries, discarding any that are badly damaged or bad, and hull. Place in a nonreactive saucepan with a lid; add the lemon juice and water. Bring to the boil, reduce to a simmer and cover with the lid. Cook for 30 minutes, or until the blackberries are soft. Stir occasionally. Cool for 5 minutes.

When cool, pour into a jelly bag and leave in a cool, draught-free place for the juice to drip through. Cover with a clean tea towel.

When all the juice has dripped through, measure the juice and pour into a preserving pan. Add the measured sugar, and crème de cassis if using.

Cook, stirring frequently, until the sugar has dissolved. Bring to a rapid boil and boil for 5-8 minutes until the setting point is reached. Draw off the heat and cool before pouring into warm sterilised jars and covering with a waxed disc. When cold, secure with a lid and label.

Cook's Tip

Do not squeeze the jelly bag or the jelly will become cloudy.

Crab Apple Jelly

Fills about 4 x 225 g/ 8 oz jars

1.75 kg/4 lb crab apples
1.7 litres/3 pints water
3-4 whole cloves
allow 450 g/1 lb preserving sugar for every 600 ml/1 pint extracted juice

Thoroughly wash the crab apples and cut into quarters. There is no need to peel or core the crab apples. Place in a large, nonreactive saucepan with a lid, and add the water and cloves. Bring to the boil, then reduce the heat before covering with the lid. Cook for 1 hour, or until the crab apples are very soft. Remove and mash with a potato masher or wooden spoon.

Pour into a jelly bag and leave in a cool, draught-free place for the juice to drip through. Cover with a clean tea towel.

When all the juice has dripped through, measure and pour into a preserving pan. Measure the sugar and add to the pan.

Cook gently, stirring frequently, for 8-10 minutes until setting point is reached. Draw off the heat and cool before pouring into warm sterilised jars and covering with a waxed disc. When cold, secure with a lid and label.

Cook's Tip

Replace the cloves with 2-3 star anise or 50 g/2 oz chopped root ginger.

Three Currant Jelly

č

Fills about 6 x 225 g/ 8 oz jars

1.75 g/4 lb mixed currants, such as blackcurrants, redcurrants and white currants, or pink if available
2.25 litres/4 pints water
4 tbsp lemon juice
thinly pared lemon zest from 1 scrubbed organic lemon
allow 450 g/1 lb preserving sugar for every 600 ml/1 pint extracted juice

Wash the currants, discarding any that are badly damaged or bad. Place in a nonreactive saucepan with a lid, add the water, lemon juice and zest; bring to the boil. Simmer and cover with the lid. Cook for 20 minutes, or until the currants are soft.

Carefully pour into a jelly bag and leave in a cool, draught-free place for the juice to drip through. Cover with a clean tea towel.

When all the juice has dripped through, measure the juice and pour into a preserving pan. Add the sugar.

Cook gently, stirring frequently, until the sugar has dissolved. Bring to a rapid boil and boil for 3-5 minutes until setting point is reached. Draw off the heat and cool before pouring into warm sterilised jars and covering with a waxed disc. When cold, secure with a lid and label.

Cook's Tip

There is no need to remove the stalks when cooking the fruit.

Cranberry Jelly

Fills about 4 x 225 g/
8 oz jars

900 g/2 lb fresh cranberries
2 large oranges, preferably
unwaxed or organic
1 lemon, preferably unwaxed
or organic
900 ml/1½ pints water
allow 450 g/1 lb preserving
sugar per 600 ml/1 pint liquid

Pick over the cranberries, wash and place in a preserving pan. Cut the oranges and lemon into wedges; add to the cranberries. Add the water, bring to the boil and simmer for 45 minutes, or until the cranberries are really soft and pulpy. Strain through a jelly bag.

Once all the juice has been extracted, measure and place in a preserving pan together with the measured preserving sugar.

Place over a gentle heat and cook, stirring frequently until the sugar has dissolved. Bring to the boil and boil rapidly for 15 minutes, or until setting point is reached. Cool slightly and skim if necessary, then pot and cover in the usual way.

Cook's Tip

For a spicy flavour, add 2-3 whole cloves and 2 tablespoons finely grated orange zest when simmering the fruits.

Thick Tomato Jelly

❦

Fills about 3 x 450 g/ 1 lb jars

900 g/2 lb unblemished, firm, ripe
tomatoes, rinsed and chopped
1 large orange, preferably unwaxed
or organic, unpeeled
2 lemongrass stalks,
roughly chopped
5 cm/2 inch piece root
ginger, chopped
1-2 whole star anise
3 whole cloves
3 tbsp white wine vinegar
900 ml/1¹/₂ pints water
allow 450 g/1 lb preserving sugar
per 600 ml/1 pint liquid
2 tbsp tomato purée
2 firm, ripe tomatoes, seeded
and chopped

Cook's Tip

Vary the spices according
to taste.

Place the tomatoes in a nonreactive
saucepan. Chop the orange, then add to
the pan with all the spices, water and
vinegar. Cook gently and bring to the
boil. Cover, then simmer for 40-50 minutes
until the tomatoes are soft and pulpy.
Cool slightly before straining through
a jelly cloth.

Measure the extract and sugar, then place
in a preserving pan. Heat gently, stirring
frequently until the sugar has dissolved,
then stir in the tomato purée.

Bring to a rapid boil and cook for 10-20
minutes until setting point is reached.
Remove from the heat, cool for at least
5 minutes, skim, then stir in the chopped
tomatoes. Pot, cover and label in the
usual way.

Blueberry Jelly

℃

Fills about 5 x 225 g/
8 oz jars

900 g/2 lb blueberries
4 ripe limes, preferably organic
1 lemon, preferably organic
2 cinnamon sticks,
lightly bruised
900 ml/1^{1}/$_{2}$ pints water
allow 450 g/1 lb preserving
sugar per 600 ml/1 pint liquid

Pick over the blueberries, wash and place in a preserving pan. Scrub the limes and lemon, cut into wedges and add to the blueberries with the cinnamon sticks and water. Bring to the boil and simmer for 20 minutes, or until the blueberries are really soft and pulpy. Strain through a jelly bag.

Once all the juice has been extracted, measure and place in the preserving pan together with the measured preserving sugar.

Place over a gentle heat and cook, stirring frequently, until the sugar has dissolved. Bring to the boil and boil rapidly for 15 minutes, or until setting point is reached. Cool slightly and skim if necessary, then pot and cover in the usual way.

Cook's Tip

When potting jams or jellies, care must be taken to ensure that the hot jam or jelly does not overflow the jars. When filled and the jars have cooled, wipe the outside of the jars with a hot, soapy cloth to clean.

Rose Petal Jelly

Fills about 3 x 225 g/ 8 oz jars

1 litre/1³/₄ pints water
350 g/12 oz just-picked rose petals
275 g/10 oz jam sugar
2 tbsp lemon juice
375 ml/13 fl oz liquid pectin
1 tbsp rose water

Soak the petals as described in the Cook's Tip. Drain, then place the petals in a nonreactive saucepan, cover with 475 ml/16 fl oz of the water, adding more if the petals are not completely covered. Bring to the boil, reduce the heat to a simmer and cover with the lid. Simmer for 30 minutes, stirring occasionally.

Remove from the heat and strain the water into a preserving pan or large, clean saucepan. Discard the petals. Add the sugar with the lemon juice and heat gently, stirring frequently, until the sugar has dissolved.

Bring to the boil and boil for 2 minutes. Add the liquid pectin and rose water. Return to the boil and boil for a further 2 minutes. Remove from the heat and leave for 5 minutes to cool. Pot and label in the usual way.

Cook's Tip

Choose rose petals that have not been sprayed with chemicals. Cut off the white part at the base of each petal. Place in a bowl and cover with water. Leave for at least 8 hours in a cool place.

Rhubarb ❧ Redcurrant Jelly

Fill about 4 x 175 g/ 6 oz jars

450 g/1 lb rhubarb
225 g/8 oz redcurrants
2 litres/3$^{1}/_{2}$ pints water
allow 450 g/1 lb preserving
sugar for each 600 ml/
1 pint juice

Trim the rhubarb, discarding the leaves, which are poisonous, and the bottom of each stalk; wash well and roughly chop. Wash the redcurrants and remove any leaves. Place both fruits in a nonreactive saucepan with a lid. Add the water.

Slowly bring to the boil. Reduce the heat to a simmer and cover with the lid. Cook gently for 15–20 minutes until soft and pulpy. Cool for 5 minutes, then strain through a jelly bag.

Once all the juice has been extracted, measure and place in a preserving pan together with the measured preserving sugar.

Cook's Tip

You can use either variety of rhubarb for this recipe. Use the forced rhubarb for a pink colour and delicate flavour. Use the green and red variety for a darker colour and more robust flavour.

Place over a gentle heat and cook, stirring frequently, until the sugar has dissolved. Bring to the boil and boil rapidly for 15 minutes, or until setting point is reached. Cool slightly and skim if necessary. Pot and cover in the usual way.

Raspberry ✿ Apple Jelly

Fills about 5 x 175 g/ 6 oz jars

700 g/1^1/$_2$ lb Bramley cooking apples
1.1 litres/2 pints water
450 g/1 lb raspberries
pared zest of 2 medium oranges
4 tbsp orange juice
allow 450 g/1 lb preserving sugar per 600 ml/1 pint of liquid

Wash the apples and discard the stalks (do not peel or core), chop, then place in a preserving pan with the water. Bring to the boil and simmer for 30 minutes. Add the raspberries and the orange zest and juice and continue to simmer for a further 30 minutes, or until the apples are very soft and pulpy. Mash the apples and raspberries together.

Cool slightly before straining through a jelly bag. Once all the juice has been extracted, measure and pour into a preserving pan and add the sugar.

Place over a gentle heat and cook, stirring frequently, until the sugar has completely dissolved. Bring to the boil and boil rapidly for 10-15 minutes until setting point is reached. Remove and cool for at least 5 minutes.

Cook's Tip

Make this recipe for a special occasion and replace the orange juice with brandy or Cointreau.

Skim if necessary, then pot, cover and label in the usual way.

Elderberry Jelly

Fills about 4 x 175 g/
6 oz jars

900 g/2 lb elderberries
900 g/2 lb cooking apples
1 large orange, preferably
organic
900 ml/1¹/₂ pints water
allow 450 g/1 lb preserving
sugar per 600 ml/1 pint liquid

Cook's Tip

Elderberries are from elderflowers, which are the flowers of small trees or shrubs that can be found in hedgerows throughout the UK and Northern Europe. In the spring, clusters of creamy white flowers can be found, which then turn into small black, blue or red berries.

Pick over the elderberries and wash thoroughly. Wash the apples and chop without coring. Place the fruits in two separate pans and cover each with half the water.

Cut the orange into wedges and add half to each pan. Bring to the boil. Simmer for 30 minutes, or until the fruits are really soft and pulpy. Strain both together through a jelly bag.

Measure the juice and place in a preserving pan with the preserving sugar.

Cook gently, stirring frequently, until the sugar has dissolved. Bring to the boil and boil rapidly for 15 minutes, or until setting point is reached. Cool slightly and skim if necessary, then pot and cover in the usual way.

Sweet Rose Hip Jelly

🍒

Fills about 4 x 175 g/ 6 oz jars

900 g/2 lb fresh rose hips
1 small orange, preferably
unwaxed or organic
1 lemon, preferably unwaxed
or organic
2 litres/3$^{1}/_{2}$ pints water
allow 450 g/1 lb preserving
sugar per 600 ml/1 pint liquid

Cook's Tip

Rose hips are best gathered
after the first frost.

Helpful Hint

As the rose hips are strained
through a jelly bag, there is
no need to remove the little
hairs on the buds.

Pick over the rose hips, discarding any that
are badly damaged, and cutting off the tops
and base. Wash and place in a nonreactive
saucepan. Scrub the orange and lemon and cut
into wedges, then add to the rose hips. Add
the water, bring to the boil and simmer for
1 hour, or until they are really soft. Strain
through a jelly bag.

Once all the juice has been extracted, measure
and place in a preserving pan together with
the measured preserving sugar.

Place over a gentle heat and cook, stirring
frequently, until the sugar has dissolved.
Bring to the boil and boil rapidly for
15 minutes, or until setting point is
reached. Cool slightly and skim if necessary,
then pot and cover in the usual way.

Aromatic Apple Jelly

ℰ

Fills about 3 x 225 g/ 8 oz jars

700 g/1½ lb Bramley cooking apples
1.1 litres/2 pints water
4 star anise
6 green cardamom pods
2 lemongrass stalks
1 small red chilli
allow 450 g/1 lb preserving sugar per 600 ml/1 pint liquid

Wash the apples and discard the stalks (do not peel or core). Chop, then place in a preserving pan with the water. Cut out a small square of muslin and place the star anise in the centre. Crack open the cardamom pods, cut the lemongrass into pieces and chop the chilli. Place with the star anise and tie up with a long piece of string. Tie to the handle of the pan. Bring to the boil and simmer for 1 hour, or until the apples are very soft.

Cool slightly before straining through a jelly bag. Once all the juice has been extracted, measure and pour into a preserving pan and add the sugar.

Place over a gentle heat and cook, stirring frequently, until the sugar has completely dissolved. Bring to the boil and boil rapidly for 10-15 minutes until setting point is reached. Remove the spices and cool for at least 5 minutes.

Cook's Tip

Make sure your spices are fresh for optimum flavour.

Skim if necessary, then pot and label in the usual way.

Rose-coloured Quince Jelly

Fills about 4 x 200 g/
7 oz jars

1.5 kg/3 lb quince
3 ripe limes, preferably organic
1 lemon, preferably organic
1.1 litres/ 2 pints water
allow 450 g/1 lb preserving
sugar per 600 ml/1 pint liquid

Cook's Tip

Quince has an aromatic
flavour when ripe, but is not
attractive with a lumpy yellow
skin. It is related to the
apple and pear and is pear
shaped. Not recommended to eat
raw as it is rather bitter.
Quince jelly makes a good
accompaniment to cheese.

Wash the quince, chop and place in a
preserving pan. Scrub the limes and lemon,
cut into wedges, and add to the preserving
pan on top of the quince and also add some
of the water. Bring to the boil and simmer
for 1 hour, or until really soft and pulpy.

Stir in the remaining water and strain
through a jelly bag. Once all the juice has
been extracted, measure and pour into the
preserving pan with the measured sugar.

Place over a gentle heat and cook, stirring
frequently, until the sugar has dissolved.
Bring to the boil and boil rapidly for
5-10 minutes until setting point is reached.
Cool slightly and skim if necessary, then
pot and cover in the usual way.

Traditional
Marmalades

Marmalade is perfect on toast and homemade marmalades are especially great on artisan breads. Here, you will find bitter fruit-peel recipes such as Traditional Chunky Marmalade, and Whisky-flavoured Marmalade, with its little bit of extra kick, for those with bolder tastes. The more unusual recipes, such as spicy Ginger Marmalade or Pink Grapefruit Marmalade, are particularly adventurous.

Traditional Chunky Marmalade

Fills about 9 x 450 g/
1 lb jars

1.5 kg/3 lb Seville oranges
juice of 2 large lemons,
preferably organic
3.4 litres/6 pints water
2.75 kg/6 lb preserving sugar
1 tsp butter

Cook's Tip

Seville oranges are grown
exclusively for marmalade
making, as they are very tart
and should not be eaten raw.
They are only available in
January and early February.
They freeze well, so buy and
freeze for use later, if liked.

Wash the oranges and cut in half. Squeeze out all the juice, scoop out all the pips from the orange shells and tie the pips up in a small piece of muslin.

Slice the peel into small chunks or strips and place in a preserving pan together with the orange and lemon juice and water. Add the pips.

Simmer gently for 1½ hours, or until the peel is very soft and the liquid has reduced by half. Remove the bag of pips, carefully squeezing to remove any juice.

Stir in the sugar and butter and heat, stirring, until the sugar has thoroughly dissolved. Bring to the boil and boil rapidly for about 15 minutes until setting point is reached. Pot, label and cover in the usual way.

Whisky-flavoured Marmalade

Fills about 9 x 450 g/
1 lb jars

900 g/2 lb Seville oranges
4 large eating oranges
2 large lemons, preferably
organic
3.4 litres/6 pints water
2.75 g/6 lb preserving sugar
300 ml/½ pint whisky
1 tsp butter

Cook's Tip

Use a blended whisky, not
a single malt. The rapid
boiling will boil off
the alcohol and leave a
delicious whiskey flavour.

Wash both kinds of orange, remove the peel
from half the oranges and cut into small
pieces. Squeeze out the juice and scoop out
the pips from all the oranges and the lemons.
Tie the pips up in a piece of muslin.

Place the peel with the orange and lemon
juice and the water into a preserving pan,
then tie the pips to the pan handle, making
sure it is covered by the water.

Simmer gently for 1½ hours, or until the peel
is very soft and the liquid has reduced by
half. Remove the bag of pips, carefully
squeezing to remove any juice.

Stir in the sugar and heat, stirring, until
the sugar has thoroughly dissolved. Add the
whisky and butter. Bring to the boil and boil
rapidly for about 15 minutes until setting
point is reached. Skim if necessary, then
cool for 5 minutes. Pot, label, and cover
in the usual way.

Lime Marmalade

Fills about 5 x 450 g/
1 lb jars

700 g/1^1/$_2$ lb limes, preferably
unwaxed or organic
4 large lemons, preferably
unwaxed or organic
1.7 litres/3 pints water
1.8 kg/4 lb preserving sugar
1 tsp butter

Cut all the fruits in half and remove all the pips. Cut out a small square of muslin, place the pips on the muslin and tie up with a long piece of string. Reserve. Squeeze out the juice.

Cut all the fruits into small pieces and place in a preserving pan with the pips tied to the pan handle. Add the juice. Add the water, then bring to the boil. Reduce to a simmer. Cook for 1½ hours, or until very soft.

Add the sugar and heat gently until the sugar has dissolved. Bring to the boil and boil rapidly for 15 minutes, or until setting point is reached. Stir in the butter. Cool slightly, then pot, label and cover in the usual way.

Cook's Tip

Choose limes that yield easily when squeezed and are bright green. Hard fruits that do not yield to a gentle squeeze will not have much juice. Try adding 2-3 peeled and chopped firm kiwis at the end of the cooking process.

Marmalade Shred Jelly

**Fills about 4 x 450 g/
1 lb jars**

1.5 kg/3 lb lemons and oranges,
preferably unwaxed or organic
1.7 litres/3 pints water
allow 450 g/1 lb preserving
sugar to each 600 ml/1 pint
extracted liquid

Cook's Tip

If liked, the fruit peel can be
chopped after simmering in the
water, with a very sharp cook's
knife or vegetable cleaver.

Peel half the fruits very thinly and cut into very fine shreds. Cover with 600 ml/1 pint of the water and simmer for 30 minutes, or until soft. Drain and reserve.

Cut all the fruits into small wedges and place in a preserving pan with any pips and the remaining water. Place over a gentle heat and bring to the boil. Reduce the heat, cover with a lid and simmer for about 1½ hours until soft.

Cool slightly, then strain through a jelly bag. Measure the strained juice and return to the preserving pan, adding the sugar for each 600 ml/1 pint liquid. Simmer until the sugar has dissolved. Bring to the boil and boil rapidly for 15 minutes, or until setting point is reached. Cool slightly, then stir in the reserved shredded peel. Pot, label and cover in the usual way.

Ginger Marmalade

Fills about 3 x 450 g/
1 lb jars

4 limes, preferably organic
2 large lemons, preferably
unwaxed or organic
50 g/2 oz piece root
ginger, chopped
1.1 litres/2 pints water
2 tsp ground ginger
900 g/2 lb preserving sugar
125 g/4 oz stem ginger, chopped

Cook's Tip

Use the freshest possible root ginger to get the maximum flavour. It needs to feel reasonably soft, not hard and brittle. Substitute oranges, if liked.

Cut off and discard both ends from the limes and lemons, then wash thoroughly. Place in a large pan with a tight-fitting lid, together with the chopped root ginger and the water. Bring to the boil; reduce the heat to a simmer. Cover with the lid and simmer for 1½ hours, or until the fruits are soft.

Cool slightly, drain off the liquid and reserve. Slice the fruits as thinly as possible, discarding the pips as you slice.

Place the slices in a preserving pan, together with the reserved liquid and the ground ginger. Add the sugar; heat gently, stirring frequently, until the sugar has dissolved.

Bring to the boil and boil steadily for about 15 minutes until setting point is reached. Cool for 5 minutes, then stir in the stem ginger. Pot, cover and label in the usual way.

Pink Grapefruit Marmalade

Fills about 6 x 450 g/
1 lb jars

3 large pink grapefruit
5 large lemons, preferably
organic
1.7 litres/3 pints water
1.5 kg/3 lb preserving sugar

Thoroughly wash the grapefruit and lemons and dry before removing the peel with a vegetable peeler, then slice finely. Cut the fruits in half; scoop out the pips. Place the pips on a small square of muslin and tie up with a long piece of string.

Place the peel in a preserving pan and tie the pip bag to the pan handle. Discard the white pith on the fruit flesh, then cut the flesh into small chunks. Add to the pan with any juice that has come out and add the water.

Bring to the boil, then reduce the heat to a simmer and cook for 1-1½ hours until the peel is very soft. Stir occasionally.

Add the sugar to the pan and cook gently, stirring occasionally, until the sugar has dissolved.

Cook's Tip

Use yellow or red or even a combination of all three coloured grapefruit.

Bring to a full rolling boil and boil for 10-15 minutes until setting point is reached. Remove from the heat and cool for at least 5 minutes, then pot, cover and label in the usual way.

Reduced-sugar Orange Marmalade

**Fills about 5 x 450 g/
1 lb jars**

1.5 kg/3 lb oranges, preferably
organic, washed or scrubbed
450 g/1 lb mandarins, preferably
organic, washed
2.25 litres/4 pints water
1.25 kg /2¹/₂ lb preserving
sugar

Thinly remove the peel from half the fruit, then shred. Cover with 900 ml/1½ pints of the water and simmer for 30 minutes.

Peel the remaining fruit and cut all the fruits in half, discarding the bitter white pith. Reserve the pips and tie up in a piece of muslin with the rest of the peel. Cut the fruit flesh into chunks and place in a large pan with the remaining water and muslin bag.

Bring to the boil, cover with a lid and reduce the heat. Simmer for 1 hour, or until the fruits are really soft. Discard the muslin bag. Transfer to a preserving pan. Stir in the sugar, then heat, stirring, until the sugar has dissolved.

Bring to the boil and boil rapidly for 15 minutes, or until setting point is reached. Draw off the heat, cool for 5-8 minutes, then stir in the reserved shredded peel. Pot, label and cover in the usual way.

Cook's Tip

Other citrus fruits can be used in this recipe if liked.

Orange ❧ Kiwi Marmalade

**Fills about 2 x 450 g/
1 lb jars**

1.5 kg/3 lb oranges, preferably
unwaxed and organic
5 cm/2 inch piece root ginger,
washed and chopped
6 kiwi fruits, peeled
and chopped
1.7 litres/3 pints water
1.75 kg/4 lb preserving sugar
1 tsp butter

Wash the oranges and peel thinly. Reserve.
Cut the fruit in half and squeeze out all
the juice. Scoop out the pips. Tie the pips
and chopped ginger up in a small piece of
muslin. Tie to the pan handle. Finely
shred the orange peel and place in a
preserving pan.

Peel the kiwi fruits, chop and add to the
pan together with the water.

Bring to the boil, then simmer gently for
1 hour. Remove the pips and discard. Stir
in the sugar and heat, stirring until the
sugar has dissolved. Add the butter.

Bring to the boil and boil rapidly for
about 15 minutes, or until setting point is
reached. Draw off the heat, cool slightly,
then stir in the reserved shredded orange
peel. Pot and cover in the usual way.

Cook's Tip
If liked, add a little finely
chopped stem ginger to the pan
once setting point is reached
and the marmalade has cooled
and is ready to pot.

Seville Orange ❧ Honey Marmalade

Fills about 5 x 450 g/ 1 lb jars

1.5 kg/3 lb Seville oranges, preferably unwaxed and organic
450 g/1 lb lemons, preferably unwaxed and organic
2.25 litres/4 pints water
900 g/2 lb preserving sugar
6 tbsp clear honey

Cook's Tip

Other citrus fruits can be used in this recipe, such as grapefruit, limes and clementines.

Thinly peel half the oranges and chop finely. Cover with 600 ml/1 pint of the water and simmer for 30 minute, then drain and reserve.

Peel the remaining oranges and cut all the fruits, including the lemons, in half. Reserve the pips and tie up in a piece of muslin together with the rest of the peel. Chop the flesh into chunks and place in a large pan together with the remaining water, and the muslin bag of pips and peel tied to the pan handle.

Bring to the boil, cover and reduce the heat and simmer for 1 hour. Discard the muslin bag. Stir in the sugar and heat, stirring frequently, until the sugar has dissolved. Stir in the honey.

Bring to a rapid boil for 15 minutes, or until setting point is reached. Draw off the heat, cool for 5-8 minutes; stir in the reserved shredded peel. Pot, label and cover in the usual way.

Lemon ❧ Ginger Marmalade

Fills about 10 x 450 g/ 1 lb jars

1.8 kg/4 lb lemons, preferably unwaxed or organic
50 g/2 oz piece root ginger, sliced
2.75 litres/5 pints water
2.25 kg/5 lb preserving sugar
225 g/ 8 oz crystallised ginger, finely chopped

Discard the stem ends from the lemons, then cut them in half and remove all the pips. Cut out a square of muslin and place the pips together with the sliced root ginger on the muslin and tie up with a long piece of string. Reserve. Squeeze out the juice.

Cut all the lemon halves into small pieces and place in a preserving pan with the pips tied to the pan handle. Add the juice. Add the water, then bring to the boil. Reduce to a simmer. Cook for 1½ hours, or until very soft.

Add the sugar and heat gently until the sugar has dissolved. Bring to the boil and boil rapidly for 15 minutes, or until setting point is reached. Stir in the crystallised ginger, cool slightly, then pot, label and cover in the usual way.

Cook's Tip

Look for lemons that are plump and firm, not hard to the touch, and that are a good colour.

Curds, Cheeses

Butters

Sticky sweet curd is everyone's favourite. Traditionally used to top desserts, curd can also be a spread for toast or bread. In addition to classic Lemon Curd, you'll also find Mixed Citrus Curd here. Using similar techniques to jam, preserve and jelly recipes, Damson Cheese and fruit butters, such as Orange and Passion Fruit Butter, are a great way to show off your new preserve-making skills.

Sweet Lemon Curd

Fills about 3 x 225 g/
8 oz jars

4 large, ripe lemons, preferably
unwaxed and organic
4 medium eggs, beaten
125 g/4 oz unsalted
butter, diced
450 g/1 lb granulated sugar

Wash or scrub the lemons and dry thoroughly. Finely grate the zest from the lemons and squeeze out all the juice. Place the zest and juice in a heatproof bowl. Stir in the eggs and then add the butter and sugar.

Place over a pan of gently simmering water, ensuring that the base of the bowl does not touch the water. Using a wooden spoon, cook, stirring constantly, until the sugar has dissolved, then continue to cook, stirring frequently, until the mixture thickens and coats the back of the wooden spoon.

Spoon into warm sterilised jars and cover the tops with waxed discs. When completely cold, cover with a lid, label and store in a cool, dark place. Use within 3 months and, once opened, store in the refrigerator.

Cook's Tip

Other fruits can be used in this recipe. Try adding the flesh and seeds of a ripe passion fruit to the mixture when adding the sugar.

Apple ❦ Apricot Curd

Fills about 3 x 225 g/ 8 oz jars

450 g/1 lb cooking apples,
peeled, cored and chopped
125 g/4 oz ready-to-eat dried
apricots, chopped finely
150 ml/¼ pint water
2 large oranges, preferably
unwaxed or organic
2 medium eggs, beaten
125 g/4 oz unsalted
butter, diced
125 g/4 oz caster sugar
1 cinnamon stick,
lightly bruised

Gently cook the apples and apricots in 150 ml/¼ pint water for 10-12 minutes until soft. Remove from the heat, then beat until smooth before passing through a sieve. Place the fruit pulp in a heatproof bowl placed over a pan of gently simmering water.

Finely grate the zest from one of the oranges and squeeze out the juice from both oranges to give 150 ml/¼ pint of juice. Add the zest and juice to the bowl together with the eggs, butter, sugar and cinnamon stick. Cook, stirring, until the butter and sugar have melted.

Continue to cook, stirring, until the mixture becomes thick and creamy. Remove the cinnamon stick and discard. Pot the curd in warm sterilised jars, cover and label in the usual way.

Cook's Tip

To get a smooth pulp, pass the cooked fruit through a food processor before sieving.

Thick Damson Cheese

Fills about 4 x 450 g/
12 oz jars

1.8 kg/4 lb ripe damsons
300 ml/$^{1}/_{2}$ pint water
150 ml/$^{1}/_{4}$ pint freshly squeezed
orange juice
2 tbsp finely grated orange zest
allow 350 g/12 oz granulated
sugar to each 600 ml/
1 pint pulp

Cook's Tip

Fruit cheeses should be thick
enough that, when a spoon is
put upright in a bowl of the
fruit cheese, it stands upright
and does not fall over. Other
fruits in the plum family can
be used for this recipe, such
as greengages, plums, or try
quince for a change.

Wash the damsons and cut in half and
discard the stones and any of the damsons
that are damaged or bad. Place in a
nonreactive saucepan or preserving pan.
Add the water with the orange juice and
finely grated orange zest. Cook for 12-15
minutes, stirring occasionally, until the
damsons have completely collapsed.

Sieve, then measure, the damson pulp and
return to the rinsed pan. Stir in the
sugar and heat, stirring constantly,
until the sugar has completely dissolved.
Continue to cook for a further 15-20
minutes until a thick, creamy consistency
is achieved. Pot into sterilised warm
jars, cover and label in the usual way.

Mixed Citrus Curd

Fills about 6 x 225 g/
8 oz jars

(All fruit preferably
organic or unwaxed)
2 large oranges
2 large lemons
2 ripe limes
6 medium eggs, beaten
175 g/6 oz unsalted
butter, diced
125 g/4 oz caster sugar
3-4 whole cloves (optional)

Cook's Tip

Replace the cloves with cinnamon,
star anise or cardamom seeds.
Remember to lightly bruise the
cinnamon stick or crack open
the cardamom pods to remove
the seeds.

If the fruits are not organic and are coated in a fine film of wax, using a small brush, scrub well in water to remove the wax. Allow to dry thoroughly before attempting to grate the zest.

Finely grate the zest from one orange, one lemon and one lime. Squeeze out the juice from the remaining fruits to give 175 ml/6 fl oz of juice. Place in a bowl together with the eggs, butter and sugar, and cloves if using. Place over a pan of gently simmering water. Cook, stirring frequently, until the butter and sugar have melted.

Continue to cook, stirring, until the mixture becomes thick and creamy. Remove the cloves and discard, then pot the curd in warm sterilised jars, cover and label in the usual way.

Blackcurrant Butter

Fills about 3 x 350 g/
12 oz jars

900 g/2 lb cooking apples
450 g/1 lb fresh ripe
blackcurrants
1.1 litres/2 pints clear
apple juice
300 ml/1/2 pint water and orange
juice mixed together
pared zest from 1 medium orange
allow 350 g/12 oz granulated
sugar each 600 ml/1 pint
of pulp

Wash, then chop, the apples into small chunks (do not peel or core), discarding any damaged pieces, and place in a preserving pan. Strip the blackcurrants off the stalks, then place in the preserving pan with the apple juice and orange water. Add the pared orange zest.

Bring to the boil, then reduce the heat and simmer gently for 30 minutes, stirring occasionally, or until the apples have completely collapsed.

Sieve, then measure, the apple and blackcurrant pulp and return to the rinsed pan. Stir in the sugar and heat, stirring constantly until the sugar has completely dissolved. Continue to cook for a further 15-20 minutes until a thick, creamy consistency is achieved. Pot into sterilised warm jars, cover and label in the usual way.

Cook's Tip

Fruit butters were traditionally made in times of glut for use straight away, as they do not keep as long as jams.

Spiced Apple Butter

1.5 kg/3 lb cooking apples
1.1 litres/2 pints apple juice
300 ml/1/2 pint water and lemon
juice mixed together
3-4 star anise
4-6 green cardamom pods
pared zest of 1 lemon
allow 350 g/12 oz granulated
sugar each 600 ml/1 pint pulp

Wash and chop the apples (do not peel or core), discarding any damaged pieces. Place in a preserving pan together with the apple juice and water. Wrap the spices and zest in a piece of muslin tied with a long piece of string. Place in the pan and tie the string to the pan handle.

Bring to the boil, then simmer gently for 30 minutes, stirring occasionally, or until the apples have completely collapsed. Discard the muslin bag.

Sieve, then measure, the apple pulp and return to the rinsed pan. Stir in the sugar and heat, stirring constantly, until the sugar has completely dissolved. Continue to cook for a further 15-20 minutes until a thick, creamy consistency is achieved. Pot into sterilised warm jars, cover and label in the usual way.

Cook's Tip

If liked, crab apples or windfall apples can be used in place of the cooking apples.

Greengage Butter

Fills about 2 x 350 g/
12 oz jars

1.5 kg/3 lb ripe greengages
600 ml/1 pint lime juice and
water mixed together
2 tbsp grated lime zest
300 ml/1/2 pint freshly squeezed
lime juice
1 tsp allspice
1 tsp ground ginger, or to taste
allow 350 g/12 oz granulated
sugar per 600 ml/1 pint pulp

Wash the greengages, cut in half and discard the stones. Place in a preserving pan with the lime juice and water. Bring to the boil. Simmer gently for 40-50 minutes until the greengages are really soft and have collapsed. Cool, then sieve, and measure the pulp in a measuring jug. Return to the cleaned pan.

Add the lime zest and juice with the ground spices. Place over a gentle heat and heat for 10 minutes. Stir in the sugar, allowing 350 g/12 oz to each 600 ml/1 pint of pulp.

Heat, stirring frequently, until the sugar has dissolved. Bring to the boil, then boil gently until the mixture has thickened and is creamy. Pot in warm sterilised jars, cover and label in the usual way.

Cook's Tip

Store in a cool, dark cupboard and use within 3 months of making. Once opened, store covered in the refrigerator.

Gooseberry Butter

Fills about 3 x 350 g/
12 oz jars

900 g/2 lb ripe gooseberries
450 g/1 lb cooking apples
1.1 litres/2 pints sweet cider
or apple juice
300 ml/½ pint water and orange
juice mixed together
2-3 strips pared orange zest
50 g/2 oz fresh root ginger,
lightly bashed
allow 350 g/12 oz granulated
sugar each 600 ml/1 pint
of pulp

Top and tail the gooseberries; reserve. Wash and chop the apples into small chunks (do not peel or core), discarding any damaged pieces, and place in a preserving pan together with the reserved gooseberries, the cider or apple juice, orange juice and water, pared orange zest and root ginger.

Bring to the boil, then reduce the heat and simmer gently for 30 minutes, stirring occasionally, or until the fruits have completely collapsed. Discard the orange zest and ginger.

Sieve, then measure, the fruit pulp and return to the rinsed pan. Stir in the sugar and heat, stirring constantly, until the sugar has completely dissolved. Continue to cook for a further 15-20 minutes until a thick, creamy consistency is achieved. Pot into warm sterilised jars, cover and label in the usual way.

Cook's Tip

Lightly bashing the ginger helps
to release the flavour.

Orange ❧ Passion Fruit Butter

Fills about 3 x 350 g/ 12 oz jars

900 g/2 lb cooking apples
450 g/1 lb small oranges (about 4)
1.1 litres/2 pints orange juice
300 ml/½ pint water
4 ripe passion fruits
allow 350 g/12 oz granulated
sugar each 600 ml/1 pint pulp

Wash and chop the apples into small chunks (do not peel or core), discarding any damaged pieces, and place in a preserving pan. Thinly peel the oranges and reserve 2-3 strips, and add to the apples. Chop the oranges; add to the pan with the orange juice and water.

Bring to the boil, then reduce the heat and simmer gently for 30 minutes, stirring occasionally, or until the apples have completely collapsed.

Sieve, then measure, the apple pulp and return to the rinsed pan together with the passion fruit pulp and seeds. Stir in the sugar and heat, stirring constantly, until the sugar has completely dissolved. Continue to cook for a further 15-20 minutes until a thick, creamy consistency is achieved. Pot into warm sterilised jars, cover and label in the usual way.

Cook's Tip

Passion fruits are ripe when they are dark, almost black and very wrinkled.

Fruity Plum Butter

Fills about 2 x 350 g/
12 oz jars

1.5 kg/3 lb ripe plums
900 ml/1^{1}/$_{2}$ pint water
2 tbsp grated orange zest
300 ml/^{1}/$_{2}$ pint freshly squeezed
orange juice
2 cinnamon sticks,
lightly bruised
allow 350 g/12 oz granulated
sugar per 600 ml/1 pint pulp

Wash the plums, cut in half and discard the stones. Place in a preserving pan with the water and bring to the boil. Simmer gently for 40-50 minutes until the plums are really soft and have collapsed. Cool, then sieve and measure the pulp in a measuring jug. Return to the cleaned pan.

Add the orange zest and juice with the cinnamon sticks and heat for 10 minutes; stir in the sugar. Heat, stirring frequently, until the sugar has dissolved. Bring to the boil, then boil gently until the mixture has thickened and is creamy. Discard the cinnamon sticks. Pot in warm sterilised jars, cover and label in the usual way.

Cook's Tip

Fruit butters do not keep well, so it is recommended that they are made in small quantities so that they are used quickly. Fruits best for making butters are blackcurrants, quinces, plums and cooking apples.

Sweet and Spicy

Chutneys

For the cheese lover, chutney is a natural counterpart to an increasingly huge range of available cheeses, and all of the recipes here provide a delicious focal point for the perfect cheese sandwich. The possibilities don't end there, however! Banana and Date Chutney is a great exotic side to many savoury dishes, and Green Tomato Chutney is a versatile 'must-have' for any picnic hamper.

Everyday Spiced Vinegar

**Makes 750 ml/
1^1/$_4$ pints**

6 tsp peppercorns
3 tsp mustard seeds
2 tsp allspice
1 blade mace
1 large cinnamon stick, bruised
4 fresh bay leaves
1 small piece root
ginger, chopped
1 tbsp salt
750 ml/1^1/$_4$ pints malt vinegar

This is an essential ingredient for making chutneys. Tie all the spices into a piece of muslin and place in a nonreactive saucepan. Add 230 ml/8 fl oz of the vinegar and bring to the boil.

Add the remaining vinegar and boil for a further 3 minutes.

Remove from the heat and leave covered for at least 24 hours. Strain into sterilised bottles and screw the caps on tightly.

Cook's Tip

Experiment with types of vinegar; distilled white wine vinegar, for example, gives a sharper tang.

Mango, Apricot & Cranberry Chutney

Makes about 1.5 kg/3 lb

8 ripe but still firm mangoes
450 g/1 lb fresh apricots
225 g/8 oz fresh cranberries
$\frac{1}{2}$ tsp salt
450 g/1 lb peeled and
chopped onions
2-4 green chillies, seeded
and chopped
3 garlic cloves, peeled
and chopped
7.5 cm/3 inch piece root
ginger, grated
450 ml/^{3}/$_4$ pint cider vinegar
550 g/1 lb 3 oz soft light
brown sugar
juice of 1 large lemon

Cook's Tip

You can vary the flavour of this chutney by using different fruits and vinegars. Simply use this as your basic recipe.

Peel the mangoes, discard the stones and roughly chop the flesh. Place in a nonreactive preserving, or large, pan. Stone the apricots, chop roughly and add to the pan together with all the remaining ingredients.

Place over a gentle heat and heat until the sugar has completely dissolved, stirring occasionally.

Bring to the boil, reduce the heat to a simmer and cook for 1 hour, or until really soft and a thick consistency is reached. Taste and adjust sweetness, then put in warm sterilised jars. When cold, cover, label and store in a cool, dark place for 1 month before using.

Red Tomato Chutney

Fills about 4 x 450 g/ 1 lb jars

1.5 kg/3 lb firm, ripe tomatoes
1 tbsp mustard seeds
1 tbsp whole allspice
1/2-1 tsp crushed chillies
225 g/8 oz onions, peeled and chopped
2-3 garlic cloves, peeled and chopped
240 ml/8 fl oz water
450 g/1 lb demerara sugar
450 ml/3/4 pint malt vinegar

Make a cross on top of each tomato; place in a large, heatproof mixing bowl. Cover with boiling water and leave for 2-3 minutes. Drain, peel, then chop the tomatoes.

Meanwhile, dry fry all the spices in a nonstick frying pan for 2-3 minutes until they pop. Remove, cool, then wrap in a small piece of muslin and tie with a long piece of string to the pan handle.

Place the tomatoes in a preserving pan with the onions and garlic. Add the water, then place over a gentle heat. Cook gently for 30 minutes, or until the tomatoes have collapsed. Stir occasionally.

Add the sugar and vinegar; bring to the boil. Reduce the heat and simmer for 35-45 minutes until a chutney consistency is reached. Cool slightly, discard the seeds, pot and label in the usual way.

Cook's Tip

Use coriander and fennel seeds for a change.

Classic Mango Chutney

ℰ

**Fills about 3 x 450 g/
1 lb jars**

125 g/4 oz sultanas
125 g/4 oz fresh dates, stones
removed, and chopped
1 red pepper, deseeded and chopped
2-4 green chillies, deseeded
and chopped
450 ml/³/₄ pints spiced vinegar
(see page 172)
6 large, ripe mangoes, peeled,
stoned and sliced
450 g/1 lb light muscovado sugar
2 garlic cloves, peeled and crushed
small piece fresh root
ginger, grated
1 onion, peeled and chopped
1 tbsp salt
5 tbsp lemon juice

Cook's Tip

Store in a cool place for
6 months before using.

Place the sultanas, dates, red pepper and green chillies in a glass bowl and cover with the spiced vinegar. Cover with a clean cloth or muslin and leave in a cool place for 24 hours.

Place the sultanas, dates, peppers and chillies in a large, nonreactive saucepan. Add all the remaining ingredients.

Place over a gentle heat and cook gently, stirring with a wooden spoon, until the sugar has dissolved. Bring to the boil, then reduce the heat to a simmer and cook for 1 hour, or until a thick consistency is reached. Stir occasionally.

Draw off the heat and cool for 5 minutes. Pack into warm sterilised jars. Once cold, cover with nonmetallic lids. Label.

Green Tomato Chutney

č

Fills about 6 x 450 g/ 1 lb jars

1.5 kg/3 lb green tomatoes
450 g/1 lb cooking apples
450 g/1 lb red onions, peeled and chopped
2-3 large garlic cloves, peeled and chopped
1 head celery
1 green jalapeño chilli pepper, deseeded and chopped
700 g/1^1/$_2$ lb demerara sugar
1 tsp coriander seeds, lightly pounded
150 ml/^{1}/$_4$ pint water
600 ml/1 pint malt vinegar
4 tbsp balsamic vinegar
300 g/11 oz raisins

Rinse and chop the tomatoes; place in a preserving pan. Peel, core and chop the apples, add to the pan with the onions and garlic. Trim and chop the celery, discarding the leaves, add to the pan with the chopped chilli, then stir in the sugar.

Tie the coriander seeds in a small piece of muslin with a long piece of string. Tie to the pan handle. Add the water; place over a gentle heat. Cook gently for 30 minutes, or until the tomatoes and apples have collapsed. Stir occasionally.

Add both vinegars and the raisins; return to the boil. Reduce the heat and simmer for 35-45 minutes until a chutney consistency is reached. Cool slightly, discard the coriander seeds, then pot and label.

Cook's Tip

Do not use soft or damaged tomatoes.

GREEN Tomato
Chutney

Banana ❧ Date Chutney

**Fills about 5 x 450 g/
1 lb jars**

450 g/1 lb cooking apples
4 shallots
3-4 garlic cloves
1 red chilli
6 large, ripe, but firm bananas,
peeled and chopped
350 g/12 oz soft brown sugar
350 g/12 oz unsweetened
chopped dates
2 tsp ground cinnamon
600-750 ml/1-1¼ pint
spiced vinegar
(see page 172)

Cook's Tip

Do not use very soft bananas, as
the finished chutney will not
have a good consistency. Fresh
dates are very expensive, but
dried dates work well. Remember
to remove and discard the stones.

Peel, core and chop the cooking apples.
Peel and chop the shallots and garlic
and place them all in a preserving pan.
Deseed the chilli, chop and add to the
apples together with all the remaining
ingredients.

Place over a gentle heat and cook,
stirring frequently, until the sugar has
dissolved. Bring to the boil, then reduce
the heat and simmer for 45 minutes, or
until a thick chutney consistency is
reached. Add the extra vinegar during
simmering if becoming dry. Cool slightly,
then pot and label in the usual way.

Fruity Apple Chutney

Fills about 8 x 450 g/
1 lb jars

900 g/2 lb cooking apples
450 g/1 lb onions, peeled
450 g/1 lb ripe plums
zest and juice of 2 small
oranges, preferably unwaxed
or organic
225 g/8 oz sultanas
450 g/1 lb light muscovado sugar
175 g/6 oz ready-to-eat
dried apricots
450 ml/^{3}/$_4$ pint spiced vinegar
(see page 172)
2 tbsp balsamic vinegar

Cook's Tip

When making chutney, remember to
use stainless steel, enamel or
aluminium pans. Vinegar can
impart a metallic taste if a
copper or iron pan is used.

Peel, core and chop the apples and onions.
Rinse the plums, cut in half, discard the
stones, chop and place in a preserving pan
with the apples, onions, orange zest and
juice. Cook gently for 15 minutes, stirring
frequently with a wooden spoon to prevent
the fruits from sticking to the base of
the pan.

Stir in all the remaining ingredients;
heat gently, stirring occasionally, until
the sugar has dissolved. Bring to the
boil, then simmer for 35-40 minutes until
a thick consistency is reached, stirring
occasionally during cooking.

Draw off the heat, cool slightly, then
pot, cover and label in the usual way.

Mixed Pepper Chutney

Fills about 4 x 450 g/ 1 lb jars

4 assorted coloured peppers
2 large onions, peeled and finely chopped
4 garlic cloves, peeled and chopped
450 g/1 lb cooking apples
450 g/1 lb ripe tomatoes, skinned and chopped
225 g/8 oz light muscovado sugar
1 tsp ground cloves
1 tsp ground ginger
1 tsp ground cinnamon
600 ml/1 pint spiced vinegar
(see page 172)
225 g/8 oz sultanas

Cook's Tip

Add 1-2 chopped chillies for a spicier chutney.

Deseed the peppers, cut into large chunks and place in a food processor and chop very finely. Alternatively, pass through a mincer. Place in a preserving pan with the onions and garlic. Peel, core and chop the apples, then add to the pan together with the chopped tomatoes.

Add the sugar with the spices; pour in the vinegar. Place over a gentle heat; bring to the boil. Reduce the heat to a simmer and cook for 25 minutes.

Stir in the sultanas and continue to simmer for a further 20 minutes, or until the vinegar has been absorbed and a thick consistency is reached.

Remove from the heat, allow to cool for 5 minutes, then pot in warm sterilised jars. Cover and label in the usual manner.

Apricot ❧ Ginger Chutney

Fills about 4 x 450 g/ 1 lb jars

450 g/1 lb dried apricots
300 ml/$^{1}/_{2}$ pint water
450 g/1 lb cooking apples
2 large onions, about 350 g/ 12 oz in weight
2-3 garlic cloves
1 head celery, trimmed and chopped
50 g/2 oz piece fresh root ginger
1 tsp ground cinnamon
225 g/8 oz demerara sugar
450 ml/$^{3}/_{4}$ pint spiced vinegar
(see page 172)
75 g/3 oz stem ginger, finely chopped

Cook's Tip

Ordinary dried apricots work better than the ready-to-eat varieties.

Chop the apricots; soak overnight in the 300 ml/$^{1}/_{2}$ pint water. Next day, place the apricots and soaking water in a saucepan. Cook gently for 12 minutes, or until soft, adding more water if necessary. When soft, place in a preserving pan.

Peel and chop the onions, garlic and apples. Add to the pan. Discard the celery leaves; trim each stalk. Rinse and finely chop, add to the pan with the root ginger and cinnamon. Stir in the sugar and vinegar.

Place over a gentle heat, slowly bring to the boil, then reduce heat to a simmer. Cook for 25 minutes, stirring occasionally. Add the chopped ginger and continue to cook for 20 minutes, or until a thick consistency is reached.

Cool for 5 minutes, then pot in warm sterilised jars. Cover and label in the usual way.

Marrow Chutney

ℰ

Fills about 5 x 450 g/ 1 lb jars

1 large marrow, about 1.8 kg/ 4 lb in weight
1-2 tbsp salt
300 g/11 oz onion
3 garlic cloves
450 g/12 oz cooking apples
50 g/2 oz fresh root ginger, grated
1 tsp ground cinnamon
1 tsp ground cloves
225 g/8 oz light muscovado sugar
900 ml/1^1/2 pints spiced vinegar *(see page 172)*
225 g/8 oz dried fruit, such as dates, finely chopped

Cook's Tip

Other squash can be used in this recipe, such as butternut or acorn.

Cut the marrow in half and discard the seeds and peel. Cut into small chunks. Layer in a colander, sprinkling each layer with salt. Leave for 30 minutes, then rinse the chunks and place in a preserving pan.

Peel and chop the onion, garlic and apples and add to the marrow together with the spices, sugar and vinegar. Place over a gentle heat and bring to the boil. Reduce the heat to a simmer and cook for 25 minutes, stirring occasionally.

Add the dried fruit and simmer for a further 20 minutes until the vinegar is absorbed and a thick consistency is reached.

When cooked, remove from the heat and cool for 5 minutes. Stir and pot in warm sterilised jars, cover and label.

Date &c Apple Chutney

Fills about 4 x 450 g/ 1 lb jars

1.8 kg/4 lb cooking apples
450 g/1 lb onions
1-2 red chillies
700g /1$^{1}/_{2}$ lb dried dates
2 medium oranges
2 tsp ground coriander
1 tsp ground cumin
3 tsp ground cinnamon
450 g/1 lb light muscovado sugar
600 ml/1 pint spiced Vinegar
(see page 172)

Peel and core the apples; chop into small pieces. Peel the onions and chop into an equal size to the apples. Deseed the chillies and chop. Discard stones from the dates and chop. Place them all in a preserving pan.

Finely grate the zest from 1 orange and squeeze out the juice from both. Add to the pan with the spices, sugar and vinegar.

Place over a gentle heat and cook, stirring, for 40-45 minutes until a thick chutney consistency is reached and all the vinegar is absorbed. Take care that the mixture does not catch on the base of the pan towards the end of cooking. Add a little water if this is happening. Draw off the heat and cool for 5 minutes before potting in the usual way.

Cook's Tip

Do not use eating apples to make chutneys, as they do not break down in the same way as cooking apples.

Beetroot ❧ Orange Chutney

Fills about 6 x 450 g/
1 lb jars

900 g/2 lb raw beetroot
450 g/1 lb onions
2-3 garlic cloves
675 g /1¹/₂ lb cooking apples
3 medium oranges
50 g/2 oz piece fresh root
ginger, grated
1 tbsp ground cinnamon
225 g/8 oz dried cranberries or
raisins
150 ml/¹/₄ pint orange juice
675 g/1¹/₂ lb demerara sugar
600 ml/1 pint spiced vinegar
(see page 172)

Wash the beetroot, discard the root and grate. Place in a preserving pan. Peel and finely chop the onions, garlic and apples. Add to the pan. Finely grate the zest of one orange, then peel all the oranges, divide into segments; add to the pan with the remaining ingredients.

Place the pan on a gentle heat; bring to the boil. Stir, then reduce the heat to a simmer. Cook for 35-45 minutes until the liquid has been absorbed and a chutney consistency has been reached. Stir occasionally during cooking, adding a little extra orange juice if starting to stick to the base.

Draw off the heat and cool for 5 minutes before spooning into warm sterilised jars. Cool before covering and labelling.

Cook's Tip

Do not use cooked beetroot for
this recipe.

Date ❧ Rhubarb Chutney

Fills about 4 x 450 g/
1 lb jars

1.8 kg/4 lb rhubarb
450 g/1 lb onions
1-2 green chillies
450 g/1 lb dried dates
300 g/11 oz demerara sugar
50 g/2 oz piece root
ginger, grated
1 tbsp ground cinnamon
2 tsp ground coriander
1 tsp ground cumin
300 ml/1/2 pint malt vinegar
300 ml/1/2 pint ginger ale or
use extra vinegar

Trim the rhubarb, discarding the stem end and leaves. Make a cut at the leaf end, then pull the knife downwards to remove the stringy part of the stalk. Repeat with all the rhubarb, then chop and place in a preserving pan.

Peel and chop the onions, deseed the chillies, discard the stones from the dates and chop. Add them all to the pan with the grated ginger. Stir in the remaining ingredients.

Bring to the boil, reduce the heat to a simmer and cook for 45-50 minutes until the rhubarb has collapsed and a chutney consistency is reached. Stir well during cooking to prevent the chutney from sticking to the base of the pan.

Draw off the heat and cool for 5 minutes before potting and labelling in the usual way.

Cook's Tip

Use the garden variety of
rhubarb for this recipe.

Perfect

Pickles

Pickles are full of spicy, aromatic and earthy flavours. Here, you will find exciting recipes to suit any meal, from Classic Piccalilli, perfect for a Ploughman's Lunch, to Sweet Mango and Orange Pickle for more exotic dishes, as well as the ultimate fish and chip accompaniments, Pickled Gherkins and Onions. These recipes will also encourage you to think up your own condiments.

Classic Piccalilli

Fills about 6 x 450 g/ 1 lb jars

2.75 kg/6 lb vegetables, such as marrow, cauliflower, carrots, baby onions, beans, celery and cucumber
175 g/6 oz salt
4.5 litres/8 pints water
225 g/8 oz granulated sugar
1 tbsp dry mustard powder
$1^{1}/_{2}$ tsp ground ginger
1.7 litres/3 pints white vinegar
4 tbsp plain flour
2 tbsp turmeric

Cook's Tip

Leave for a few months before using. Ideal to make when there is a glut of vegetables.

Peel and trim the vegetables, then cut into bite-sized pieces. Place in a large bowl; sprinkle with salt. Cover with the water. Leave for 24 hours.

Next day, remove the vegetables, rinse and drain. Blend the sugar, mustard powder and ground ginger with 1.5 litres/$2^{1}/_{2}$ pints of the vinegar. Place the vegetables in a preserving pan and pour over the mustard and vinegar mixture.

Bring to the boil, then reduce the heat to a simmer and cook for 20 minutes, or until the vegetables are tender but still retain a bite. Blend the flour with the remaining vinegar and the turmeric and stir into the vegetables.

Cook, stirring, for 5 minutes, or until the liquid thickens. Remove from the heat and cool for 5 minutes before potting and labelling in the usual way.

Simple Beetroot Pickle

Fills about 4 x 450 g/
1 lb jars

900 g/2 lb raw beetroot
225 g/8 oz onions, peeled and
finely chopped
450 g/1 lb Bramley cooking apples,
peeled, cored and finely chopped
grated zest and juice of 2 large
limes, preferably organic
900 ml/1$\frac{1}{2}$ pints spiced Vinegar
(see page 172)
300 ml/$\frac{1}{2}$ pint water
450 g/1 lb dark brown sugar
125 g/4 oz ready-to-eat dried
apricots, finely chopped
125 g/4 oz crystallised ginger,
finely chopped

Cook's Tip

Keep for 6 months only. Do not use
cooked beetroot, either from a
jar or vacuum packed. They do not
give good flavour or consistency.

Peel the beetroot and either grate or
finely chop. Place in a preserving pan
with the onions, cooking apples, lime
zest and juice. Add the vinegar and water
and place over a gentle heat and bring to
the boil. Reduce the heat and simmer for
15 minutes.

Add the sugar and, stirring frequently,
heat until the sugar has dissolved, then
stir in the apricots and ginger. Simmer
for 30 minutes, or until the beetroot
is soft. Cool slightly before potting,
covering and labelling in the usual way.

Sweet ❦ Hot Vegetable Pickle

Fills about 5 x 450 g/
1 lb jars

2 kg/4^{1}/$_{2}$ lb mixed vegetables,
such as cauliflower, carrots,
baby onions, celery
and broccoli
6 garlic cloves, peeled
and chopped
1-2 red chillies, deseeded
and chopped
175 g/6 oz salt
225 g/8 oz granulated sugar
1 tbsp mustard powder
1 tbsp turmeric
1.1 litres /2 pints malt vinegar
5 cm/2 in piece root
ginger, grated
3 tbsp plain flour

Peel and trim the vegetables; cut into small
pieces. Place in a large bowl with the garlic
and chillies; sprinkle with salt. Cover with
boiling water. Leave for 24 hours.

Next day, drain the vegetables and rinse in
cold water. Repeat, then place in a preserving
pan. Blend the sugar, mustard powder and
turmeric with half the vinegar. Pour over the
vegetables, stir in the ginger and place over
the heat.

Simmer for 20 minutes, or until the vegetables
are tender but still retain a bite. Blend the
flour with the remaining vinegar and stir into
the vegetables.

Cook, stirring, for 5 minutes, or until the
liquid thickens. Remove from the heat and
cool for 5 minutes before potting and
labelling in the usual way.

Cook's Tip

Keeps for up to 6 months.

Pickled Red Cabbage

1 red cabbage, 1.25 kg/2$^1/_2$ lb
in weight
salt
1.5 litres/2$^1/_2$ pints
spiced vinegar
(see page 172)

Choose firm cabbages that feel heavy and are a good colour. Cut off a slice about 1 cm/$^1/_2$ inch thick from the stalk end and discard. Remove the outside leaves and cut the cabbage into quarters. Discard the central core from each quarter. Using a very sharp knife, shred the cabbage as thinly as possible.

Using a large glass mixing bowl, arrange a layer of the shredded cabbage in the base about 2.5 cm/1 inch high. Sprinkle with a layer of salt, then cover with a further layer of cabbage and then salt. Repeat the layering until all the cabbage has been used, finishing with a layer of salt. Cover and leave overnight in a cool place.

Next day, drain, then rinse the cabbage thoroughly and shake off any excess water. Pack into sterilised jars to within 2.5 cm/1 inch of the top of each jar. Pour in sufficient spiced vinegar to cover the cabbage. Cover with nonmetallic lids.

Cook's Tip

Use within 2-3 weeks before the cabbage loses its crispness and becomes soft.

Home-made Pickled Onions

Fills about 4 x 450 g/
1 lb jars

1.8 kg/4 lb pickling onions

First brine
450 g/1 lb salt
4.5 litres/8 pints water

Second brine
450 g/1 lb salt
4.5 litres/8 pints water
spice vinegar to cover
(see page 172)

Cook's Tip

Add some extra flavour to the onions. Try adding a few whole cloves, 3-6, or, depending on your heat tolerance, chopped red chillies and include the seeds as well.

Choose small, firm onions. A pail would be the best utensil to put the onions in, but do not use a metal one. Dissolve the salt in the water to make the two brines.

Remove any loose skin and wash lightly. Do not peel the onions. Place in the pail and cover with the first brine. Leave for 12 hours.

Drain the onions and peel, return to the pail and cover with the second brine. Leave for 24-36 hours. Drain and rinse off the excess salt. Pack into jars, cover and label in the usual way. Remember not to use metal lids. Leave for at least 3 months before using.

Pickled Gherkins

Fills about 3 x 450 g/
1 lb jars

450 g/1 lb salt
4.5 litres/8 pints water
900 g/2 lb gherkins
brine, made from salt and water
4-5 whole cloves
1 tbsp black peppercorns
2 tsp whole allspice
50 g/2 oz fresh root
ginger, grated
600 ml/1 pint spiced vinegar
(see page 172)

Cook's Tip

Use within 3 months.
If liked, add 3-4 bay leaves
and the pared zest of 2 lemons
with the spices.

Wash the gherkins and place in a glass mixing bowl. Cover with brine and leave in a cool, dark place for 3 days. After 3 days, rinse thoroughly and dry, then pack into jars.

Lightly pound the whole spices in a pestle and mortar until they have been cracked open. Place in a saucepan and stir in the grated root ginger and the Spiced Vinegar. Place over a medium heat and bring to the boil. Boil for 10 minutes, then remove from the heat.

Pour the vinegar with the spices over the gherkins, ensuring that they are completely covered. Cover and leave for 24 hours in a warm place. Strain off the vinegar and boil again for 10 minutes, then use to re-cover the gherkins.

Repeat this process at least twice more until the gherkins are a good green colour. Drain again, reserving the vinegar, pack the gherkins in sterilised wide-necked jars. Pour in sufficient fresh Spiced Vinegar to cover.

Pepper Pot Pickle

Fills about 3 x 450 g/
1 lb jars

450 g/1 lb cooking apples
2 large onions, peeled and
thinly sliced
3-4 garlic cloves, peeled
and sliced
2-4 (depending on heat
tolerance) chillies, deseeded
and finely sliced
900 g/2 lb assorted coloured
peppers, deseeded and
finely chopped
450 g/1 lb light muscovado sugar
1-3 tsp, or to taste,
Tabasco sauce
350 ml/12 fl oz red wine vinegar

Cook's Tip

If a more fiery relish is liked,
use chillies that have higher
heat content, such as Bird eye
chillies or habanera.

Peel, core and chop the apples and place in
a preserving pan together with the onions,
garlic, chillies and peppers. Sprinkle with
the sugar. Add the Tabasco sauce.

Simmer gently for 15 minutes, stirring
frequently, until the apples and onions
are beginning to soften. Add the vinegar
and continue to simmer for 40 minutes, or
until a thick consistency is reached and
the liquid is absorbed.

Check the sweetness and, if necessary, add
a little extra sugar; simmer for a further
10 minutes. Draw off the heat; cool for
5 minutes before potting and labelling in
the usual way. Allow to mature for at least
1 month before using.

Sweet Mango ❧ Orange Pickle

Fills about 4 x 350 g/ 12 oz jars

4 ripe mangoes, about 900 g/ 2 lb in weight
1-2 (according to heat tolerance) red chillies, deseeded and chopped
5 cm/2 in piece root ginger, peeled and grated
grated zest and juice of 2 oranges, preferably unwaxed or organic
600 ml/1 pint water
450 g/1 lb light muscovado sugar
175 g/6 oz raisins
2-3 tbsp balsamic vinegar

Cook's Tip

Other flavours can be used if liked. Try adding 4 star anise, 6 lightly cracked cardamom pods and 2 whole cloves, tied in a small piece of muslin.

Peel, stone and finely chop the mangoes and place in a preserving pan together with the chillies and grated root ginger. Add the orange zest and juice and stir in the water. Bring to the boil and simmer for 20 minutes.

Add the sugar and raisins to the pan and heat gently until the sugar has dissolved. Bring to the boil and boil for 10 minutes, or until a thick consistency is reached. Stir in the balsamic vinegar and cook for a further 5 minutes. Cool slightly, then pot in clean sterilised jars and seal when cold.

Melon Rind Pickle

Fills about 2 x 450 g/
1 lb jars

450 g/1 lb melon rind
2 tbsp salt
1.7 litres/3 pints very
hot water
450 ml/³/₄ pint distilled vinegar
450 g/1 lb demerara sugar
3 whole star anise
6 cardamom pods, lightly cracked
2 whole cloves
300 g/11 oz dried apricots

Chop the rind into small pieces (if liked, do this in a food processor) and place in a preserving pan; sprinkle with the salt. Pour over a quarter of the very hot water. Cover and leave for 30 minutes.

Bring the melon and water to the boil; simmer for 30 minutes. Drain and rinse, then return to the pan. Cover with a further quarter of the hot water. Bring to the boil and simmer for 10 minutes. Drain, re-cover with fresh cold water. Bring to the boil and boil for 10 minutes. Remove from the heat and leave overnight.

Next day, drain the melon; return to the pan. Add the vinegar, sugar and spices tied up in a small piece of muslin. Finely chop the apricots and add to the pan.

Cook's Tip

Use within 3 months. Any melon can be used for this; try honeydew or Gallia.

Simmer gently for 1 hour, or until the melon rind is clear. Remove the spice; pot, cover and label. Leave for 2 weeks before using.

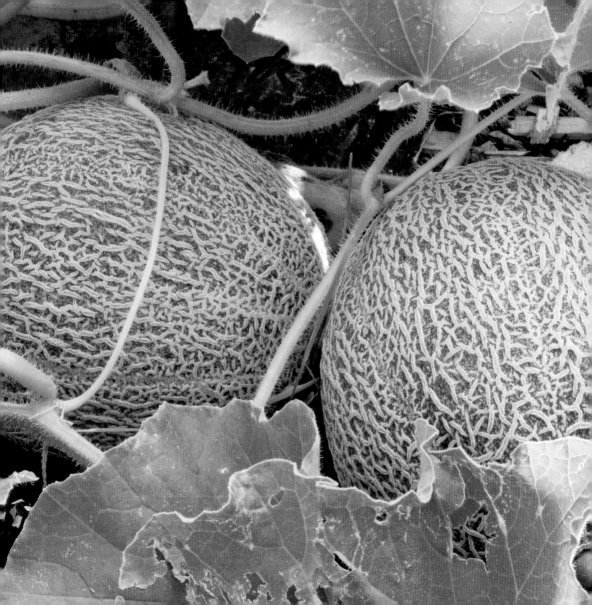

Preserved Fruit <small>&</small> Vegetables, Oils <small>&</small> Vinegars

Good preserves require a little patience, but are well worth the wait. Here, you will find recipes for delicious preserves that mature and improve over time. Once you get the hang of them, the possibilities are endless, and unusual preserves, such as Clementines in Cointreau, Rumtopf or Sweet and Sour Apricots, are great for digging out of the back of the cupboard for last-minute gifts, or just as a treat!

Make your own Vinegar Mother

Making Vinegar

2 tbsp vinegar
$^1\!/_2$ bottle red or white wine, or
cider, or ale

Cook's Tip

No cook can be without vinegar
in her store cupboard and it
is integral in the making of
chutney, pickles and preserves.
Nowadays, most people buy their
vinegar, but it is in fact very
simple to make your own.
Vinegar comes from wine or
barley and occurs when the
alcohol in the wine or barley
starts to ferment, forming
bacteria, and this is known as
the Mother from which the
vinegar is made and to which
different flavours can be added.

Place the vinegar and the alcohol in a wide-necked container, cover and leave in a sunny place for a few weeks. A skin will form which is the aceto bacteria and this is the Mother.

Skim off the Mother and place it in a wide-necked container or bowl. Add more of the same alcohol and cover with muslin. Keep in a warm place. Ensure that the mixture is able to receive plenty of oxygen.

After 1 month, strain out the vinegar. The Mother can be kept and used again and again as long as fresh alcohol is added which will feed the Mother.

Thyme Vinegar

Makes 600 ml/1 pint

450 g/1 lb fresh thyme sprigs
600 ml/1 pint white wine vinegar

Cook's Tip

This method also works well with other ingredients, such as raspberries or blackberries. Wash 450 g/1 lb berries and place half in a glass bowl and cover with 450 ml/1 pint white wine vinegar. Cover and leave for 24 hours. Strain, then pour the steeped vinegar over the remaining berries; leave for 24 hours. Strain off the vinegar and discard the berries. Place the vinegar in a saucepan and add 450 g/1 lb sugar for every 600 ml/1 pint strained vinegar. Boil for 30 minutes before cooling, then pour into bottles and seal when cold.

Rinse the thyme and pat dry. Place in a glass bowl; pour over the vinegar. Cover with a clean cloth or muslin and leave in a cool place for 2 days. Stir and leave for 7 days. Stir again and leave for 1 month.

Strain the vinegar through a very fine sieve or muslin and discard the thyme. Pour the prepared vinegar into glass bottles. Lightly rinse some fresh thyme sprigs and place in the vinegar. Secure with a cap and store in a cool, dark cupboard.

Preserved Mushrooms

Fills about 4 x 225 g/ 8 oz jars

600 ml/1 pint white wine vinegar
450 ml/³/4 pint water
1 tbsp salt
12 fresh bay leaves
6 whole cloves
8 black peppercorns
1 medium onion, peeled and thinly sliced
8 assorted chillies
900 g/2 lb assorted mushrooms, wiped and trimmed as necessary
about 600 ml/1 pint olive oil

Cook's Tip

Use within 6 months. If using wild mushrooms, wipe off any soil and trim the stalks. Gently brush the mushrooms clean. Cultivated mushrooms should not be washed. Wipe with soft kitchen paper.

Place the vinegar, water, salt, 6 of the bay leaves with half the cloves and peppercorns in a large, nonreactive saucepan. Add the onion and half the chillies. Bring to the boil and boil for 5 minutes. Reduce the heat to a simmer before adding all the prepared mushrooms.

Simmer for 5 minutes, then draw off the heat and cool for 5 minutes. Drain and place between 2 clean cloths or plenty of absorbent kitchen paper. Leave for 2-3 hours until dry.

When the mushrooms are completely dry, spoon into sterilised jars together with the remaining bay leaves, whole cloves, peppercorns and chillies. Cover completely with the olive oil. Secure with the lids, label and store in a cool, dark place, not the refrigerator.

Preserved Mixed Vegetables

Fills about 4 x 450 g/ 1 lb jars

450 g/1 lb baby aubergines
450 g/1 lb courgettes
2 tbsp salt
6 assorted peppers, about
450 g/1 lb in weight
1.5 litres/2$\frac{1}{2}$ pints white
wine vinegar
600 ml/1 pint water
6 fresh bay leaves
1 tbsp whole allspice
6 whole cloves
2 tsp black peppercorns
900 ml/1$\frac{1}{2}$ pints olive oil

Trim the aubergines and courgettes, and slice fairly thinly. Layer with salt in a colander and leave for 30 minutes. Drain, rinse to remove any excess salt and pat dry with absorbent kitchen paper.

Cut the peppers into quarters and discard the seeds. Place under a hot grill and cook for 10 minutes until the skins have blackened. Remove and place in a polythene bag. Leave until cool, then skin and slice.

Pour the vinegar and water into a nonreactive saucepan, add the bay leaves and spices. Bring to the boil. Stir in the vegetables, simmer for 5 minutes, ensuring that all the vegetables are covered with liquid. Drain, then leave on trays lined with kitchen paper overnight to dry completely.

In sterilised jars, place layers of vegetables and oil, ensuring that the vegetables are completely covered with oil. Seal and label.

Cook's Tip

Store for at least 1 month before using.

Basil Olive Oil

**Makes 2 x 300 ml/
1/2 pint bottles**

600 ml/1 pint olive oil
50 g/2 oz fresh basil leaves,
plus 4-6 extra sprigs

Cook's Tip

Other flavours can be used to make
different flavoured oils. Try
rosemary, oregano, dill, tarragon
or a combination of herbs. If you
like hot, spicy food, use some
chopped chillies. Proceed as
above, steeping 6-8 chopped
chillies in the oil and then
placing 1-3 of the very small
chillies in the oil once bottled.

Do not, however, use garlic when
flavouring oil, as it can cause
botulism. This type of flavoured
oil should only ever be
made commercially.

Lightly rinse the basil leaves; place in
a glass bowl. Pour in the olive oil, then
cover with a clean cloth or muslin. Leave
for at least 2 weeks in a cool place.

When ready to bottle, sterilise 2 x 300 ml/
1/2 pint bottles with tightly fitting lids.
Dry thoroughly. Drain the olive oil,
discarding the basil leaves. Use a funnel
to fill the bottles. Carefully insert 2-3
fresh basil sprigs and screw down tightly.

Leave for at least 1 week for the flavour
to develop. Store in a cool place, but not
the refrigerator, as this will make the
oil cloudy.

Preserved Aubergines

C

Makes about 450 g/1 lb

450 g/1 lb aubergines
2-3 tbsp salt
300 ml/$^{1}/_{2}$ pint water
300 ml/$^{1}/_{2}$ pint white wine vinegar
2 tsp whole allspice
2 tbsp black peppercorns
2 tsp capers
50 g/2 oz pitted olives
1 red chilli
2 tbsp freshly chopped coriander
300 ml/$^{1}/_{2}$ pint olive oil

Trim and slice the aubergines. Layer with 1-2 tablespoons of the salt in a colander standing on a tray to catch the water extracted. Leave for 8 hours, then remove and discard the extracted water.

Pat the aubergine slices dry with kitchen paper, place in a saucepan with the remaining salt, water, vinegar, allspice and peppercorns. Bring to the boil and reduce the heat, then simmer for 5 minutes.

Drain the aubergines, discarding the vinegar mixture. Place the aubergines on plenty of absorbent kitchen paper. Leave until completely dry, replacing the paper as necessary.

Thoroughly rinse the salt off the capers, then chop finely with the olives, chilli and coriander.

Cook's Tip

Store in a cool place.

Layer the aubergines with the chopped caper mixture in one or two glass jars with tight-fitting lids. Pour in sufficient oil to cover. Seal and store for at least 2 weeks before using.

Clementines in Cointreau

Fills about 3-4 x 450 g/ 1 lb jars

900 g/2 lb clementines
450 g/1 lb caster sugar
600 ml/1 pint water
150 ml/¼ pint Cointreau

Look for fruits that are firm to the touch and whose skin does not feel loose. This is an indication that the fruit has passed its prime.

Peel the clementines, taking care to remove all the small strands of pith and any pips. Wipe with kitchen paper to remove any excess juice. Reserve.

Place 125 g/4 oz of the sugar in a heavy-based saucepan and add 300 ml/½ pint of the water. Heat gently, stirring occasionally with a wooden spoon, until the sugar has dissolved. Bring to the boil and boil vigorously until a light syrup is formed. Reduce the heat and add the prepared fruit. Cook gently for 3-4 minutes, then remove the fruit carefully, reserving the syrup as well.

When cool, pack the fruit into glass jars. Add the remaining water and sugar to the reserved syrup and heat until the sugar has dissolved. Boil until reduced by half, remove and cool. Add the Cointreau, then pour over the fruit, cover with the lid and label.

Cook's Tip

Try using mandarins, orange slices or peeled peaches.

Boozy Rumtopf

Amounts for this recipe
are difficult to
predict, as it is made
over a number of months

450 g/1 lb ripe seasonal fruit,
such as strawberries,
raspberries, apricots
plums and grapes
450 g/1 lb granulated sugar for
the first layer
225 g/8 oz granulated sugar for
other layers
rum to cover each layer

Cook's Tip

Fruits to avoid for this recipe
are blueberries, blackberries,
melons, bananas or citrus
fruits, all of which can make
the other fruit bitter.

Choose seasonal fruits that are in perfect
condition. If large, cut into smaller pieces.
Ensure the pot you use has a wide neck for easy
arrangement of the fruits and is not metallic.
It is possible to buy pots specifically for
making Rumtopf.

Prepare the fruits (use either one variety or a
mixture), lightly rinse and pat dry. Place the
fruit in the container and cover completely with
the sugar and then add sufficient rum to cover,
so it is 2.5 cm/1 inch higher than the level of
the fruit. Cover with muslin and store in a
cool place for at least 1 month.

Repeat the layering with other seasonal fruits
and continue layering using 225 g/8 oz fruit
and sugar in the layers, not forgetting the
rum. Leave for 1 month. Repeat until the pot is
almost full and finish with the rum. Store for
at least another month before eating.

Cherries in Kirsch

Fills about 3-4 x 450 g/
1 lb jars

900 g/2 lb ripe cherries
450 g/1 lb caster sugar
600 ml/1 pint water
150 ml/1/4 pint Kirsch

Look for cherries that are firm to the touch with shiny skins. Discard any that look as if they have been pecked by birds.

Remove any stalks. If liked, the cherries can be stoned; however, the cherries will collapse and not look as attractive. Wash the cherries and pat dry. Using a darning needle or very fine skewer, prick the cherries all over. Reserve.

Place 125 g/4 oz of the sugar in a heavy-based saucepan; add 300 ml/½ pint of the water. Heat gently, stirring occasionally with a wooden spoon, until the sugar has dissolved. Bring to the boil and boil vigorously until a light syrup is formed. Reduce the heat and add the prepared cherries. Poach gently for 3-4 minutes; remove the fruit carefully, reserving the syrup as well.

When cool, pack the cherries into sterilised glass jars. Add the remaining water and sugar to the reserved syrup; cook gently until the sugar has dissolved. Boil until reduced by half, remove and cool. Add the Kirsch, then pour over the cherries; cover with the lid and then label.

Cook's Tip

Fruit preserved in an alcohol syrup make an ideal Christmas treat.

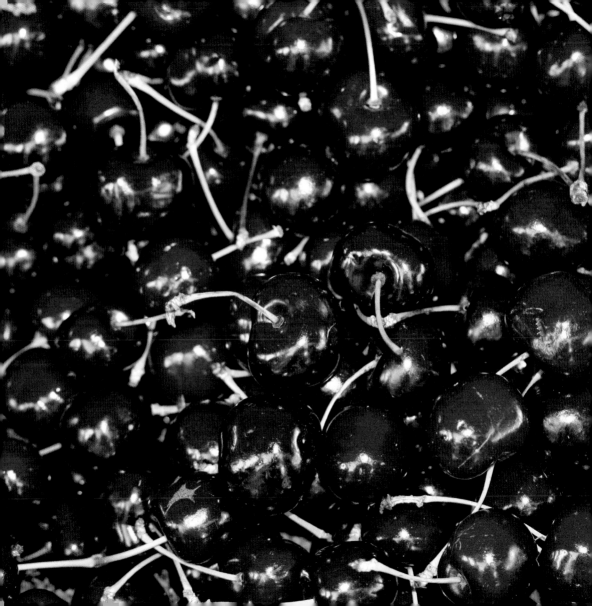

Peaches in Brandy

*

Makes 900 g/2 lb

900 g/2 lb fresh peaches
450 g/1 lb caster sugar
600 ml/1 pint water
150 ml/¼ pint brandy

Look for unblemished peaches that are almost ripe but still have a little firmness when lightly squeezed. Make a small cross in the top of each fruit and place in a heatproof glass bowl. Cover with boiling water and leave for 2-3 minutes. Drain, then carefully peel and, if liked, cut in half and discard the stone.

Place 125 g/4 oz of the sugar in a heavy-based saucepan; add 300 ml/½ pint of the water. Heat gently, stirring occasionally with a wooden spoon, until the sugar has dissolved. Bring to the boil and boil vigorously until a light syrup is formed. Reduce the heat and add the prepared peaches. Poach gently for 3-4 minutes, then remove the fruit carefully. Reserve the syrup as well.

Cook's Tip

If liked, canned peach halves can also be prepared in this way.

When cool, pack the peaches into sterilised glass jars. Add the remaining water and sugar to the reserved syrup. Cook gently until the sugar has dissolved. Boil until reduced by half, remove and cool, then pour over the brandy, cover with the lid and label.

Sweet & Sour Apricots

**Fills about 2 x 450 g/
1 lb jars**

450 g/1 lb fresh apricots
350 g/12 oz demerara sugar
600 ml/1 pint white wine vinegar
thinly pared zest of
1 small orange
4 tbsp orange juice
2 cinnamon sticks,
lightly bruised

Choose apricots that are in sound condition and are not completely ripe. Make a small cross in the top of each fruit. Rinse, then place in a glass bowl and cover with boiling water. Leave for 2-3 minutes, then drain, cool slightly and peel. Cut in half and discard the stones. Reserve.

Place the vinegar in a frying pan with the demerara sugar and pared zest of the orange, together with the orange juice and cinnamon sticks. Place over a low heat and cook gently, stirring with a wooden spoon, until the sugar has completely dissolved.

Add the apricots to the pan and gently poach for 5-10 minutes until the apricots are tender. Remove the fruit with a slotted draining spoon and pack into warm sterilised jars.

Cook's Tip

Use within 6 months.

Increase the heat under the syrup and boil until reduced by half. Discard the cinnamon sticks, then cool the syrup. Pour over the apricots. Seal and label and keep for 3 weeks before using.

Sun-dried Tomatoes

Fills about 4 small jars

900 g/2 lb ripe tomatoes
1 tbsp salt
1 tbsp caster sugar
few basil leaves, or other herbs
of your choice
about 600 ml/1 pint olive oil

Cook's Tip

Use within 6 months.

Preheat the oven to 130°C/250°F/Gas Mark $1/2$. Choose tomatoes that are ripe but still firm to the touch and blemish free. Wash the tomatoes and cut in half horizontally. Sprinkle the cut side with the salt and sugar, then arrange cut-side down on two or more baking sheets.

Place in the oven and allow to dry out very slowly. This will take at least 6-7 hours. Do not be tempted to speed up the drying-out process, as the tomatoes need enough time to dry out evenly so the flavour is increased. Start checking after 5 hours. The tomatoes will be ready when they feel dry and have a chewy texture.

When the tomatoes are dry, pack in layers in small, sterilised glass jars. Place small sprigs of basil or herbs of your choice between the layers. When the jars are full, allow 1.25 cm/$1/2$ inch of space at the top and fill with the oil, covering the tomatoes completely. Cover with the lid, seal and label.

Sweet Spiced Plums

Makes about 2 x 450 g/
1 lb jars

900 g/2 lb dessert plums
thinly pared zest and juice of
1 large orange
300 ml/¹/₂ pint spiced vinegar
(see page 172)
350 g/12 oz light
muscovado sugar
5 whole cloves
2 star anise
1 cinnamon stick,
lightly bruised
300 ml/¹/₂ pint water

Choose plums that are almost ripe and still retain some firmness when squeezed lightly. Wash plums and, if preferred, cut in half and discard the stones.

Using a large saucepan or frying pan, place the orange zest and juice with the Spiced Vinegar, the sugar and cloves, star anise and cinnamon stick. Add the water. Heat gently until the sugar has dissolved, stirring occasionally with a wooden spoon. When the sugar has dissolved, bring to the boil and boil vigorously for 10 minutes, or until a light sugar syrup is formed.

Reduce the heat to a simmer, add the plums and poach for 5-8 minutes until cooked. Draw off the heat and leave to cool for 5 minutes. Pack the plums into sterilised jars. When cool, cover and label.

Cook's Tip

Use within 1 month of making.

Mixed Vegetable Pickles

Makes 900 g/2 lb

900 g/2 lb mixed vegetables,
such as cauliflower, broccoli,
courgettes, shallots,
cucumber, French beans
and carrots
3 tbsp salt
1 litre/2 pints water
1 litre/2 pints spiced vinegar
(see page 172)

If using cauliflower or broccoli, break into small florets. Peel the shallots and cucumber and discard the seeds. Trim the beans and wash thoroughly, then chop into small pieces. Peel the courgettes and cut into small chunks. Peel the carrots and dice.

Dissolve the salt in 1 litre/2 pints water. Place all the vegetables in a large bowl and pour over the brine. Leave overnight.

Next day, rinse thoroughly at least 3-4 times to remove any excess salt, then drain and dry on clean cloths. Pack into sterilised jars and cover with the vinegar. Cover with nonreactive lids. Label and store in a cool, dark place.

Cook's Tip

All manner of vegetables can be used for these pickles. They are ideal for pickling excess vegetables when they are in season and there is a glut.

Fragrant Rose Vinegar

**Makes approx 600 ml/
1 pint**

350 g/12 oz rose petals
approx 300 ml/$^1/_2$ pint
white wine vinegar

This is a delicately flavoured vinegar
that is perfect to use as a dressing on
salads or vegetables. Lightly rinse and
dry the petals, ensuring that there are
no insects or bugs.

Place in a sterilised 300 ml/$^1/_2$ pint
glass jar with a screw-top lid. Do not
pack down too firmly.

Cover with the white wine vinegar, seal
and leave in a sunny place for at least
1 month before using.

Cook's Tip

Make sure that you use rose
petals that have a perfume.
Petals from other edible
flowers can be used in this
way too: try chrysanthemums,
nasturtiums, marigolds
or sweet peas.

Rosemary Vinegar

Makes 600 ml/1 pint

450 g/1 lb fresh rosemary
sprigs, rinsed
600 ml/1 pint white wine or
cider vinegar

Discard the woody stems from the rosemary and place half in a glass bowl. Pour over the vinegar, stir, cover lightly and leave in a cool place for 7 days, stirring occasionally.

Strain, discarding the rosemary. Repeat with the remaining rosemary and pour the strained vinegar over. Cover lightly, stir occasionally and then leave for a further 7 days.

Pour through a fine sieve into sterilised bottles. Add 2-3 rinsed fresh rosemary sprigs and screw the lids down tightly. Store in a dark place.

Cook's Tip

This recipe can be used with a variety of herbs: try tarragon, thyme, bay or oregano. The more delicate herbs, such as basil, dill, mint and coriander, will need their leaves bruising slightly. Avoid using dried herbs or spices, as these could make the vinegar cloudy.

Classic Mint Sauce

Makes 85 ml/3 fl oz

25 g/1 oz mint sprigs
2 tsp caster sugar or
clear honey
2 tbsp boiling water
2 tbsp white wine vinegar
1 tbsp balsamic vinegar

Strip off the mint leaves from the stalks and chop finely. Place in a small bowl and add the sugar or honey.

Pour over the boiling water, stir well and then leave for 5 minutes.

Add both vinegars, stir well and pour into a sauce boat. Leave for 1 hour before using.

Cook's Tip

Ideal to serve with all lamb dishes. Try adding a spoonful or two to a lamb casserole or stew.

Index

Index